WILLIAMSBURG RESEARCH STUDIES

WILLIAMSBURG RESEARCH STUDIES

The Negro
in Eighteenth-Century
Williamsburg

The Negro
in Eighteenth-Century
Williamsburg

By

THAD W. TATE

COLONIAL WILLIAMSBURG

Williamsburg, Virginia

Distributed by

THE UNIVERSITY PRESS OF VIRGINIA

Charlottesville

FOREWORD

WILLIAMSBURG RESEARCH STUDIES is a series of
specialized reports prepared in the research program of
Colonial Williamsburg. For almost forty years this program has sought to fulfill a dual objective: to supply
the day-to-day information essential to the accurate pre-
servation and restoration of Virginia's colonial capital,
and to supplement the interpretation of Williamsburg with
studies broader in scope but as detailed in content. The
series will make available in inexpensive form those studies
of widest interest to students of the era and locality.

To inaugurate the series, we have chosen seven
reports from the files of the Research Department. These
studies originally were for internal use only; some are
largely compilations of the documentary sources relating
to a subject, and others are more interpretive. Future
titles will appear as research projects are concluded and
will include contributions from the fields of architecture,
archaeology, hand crafts, and the decorative arts.

For permission to publish certain copyrighted
material in this volume, we should like to express apprecia-

tion to the Columbia University Press, New York; the

Historical Society of Pennsylvania, Philadelphia; the

Society for the Propagation of the Gospel in Foreign Parts,

London; and the University of Virginia Library, Charlottes-

ville.

Edward M. Riley
Director of Research

PREFACE

       The following study was completed initially in the spring of 1957 as a research report for Colonial Williamsburg, Inc., with the idea that it would for the most part be used by the staff of that organization in whatever way it might serve to aid in the interpretation of restored Williamsburg. The decision to make it and a number of comparable studies of eighteenth-century Williamsburg more widely available in this present series is, as I understand it, intended to preserve in large measure the original format of a research report. For this reason I have not undertaken any extensive changes in my original manuscript. I have, however, made a few revisions, especially to take into account recent work on the origins of slavery, to incorporate additional evidence on the Negro school operated in Williamsburg under the auspices of the Associates of Dr. Bray, and to make use of new statistics on Negro population in the Virginia colony. Although further research would undoubtedly add additional details to my account, I do not believe that they would substantially alter the conclusions that I have reached.

In a sense, two approaches were possible in the preparation of this study of Williamsburg's Negro population in the colonial era. One alternative would have been a broad survey of what would really amount to slavery and the Negro in Tidewater Virginia. The other would confine itself as far as possible to Williamsburg and to the impact of town life on an element in the population whose initial reason for being here had been the performance of agricultural labor.

For the most part, I have attempted to follow the narrower approach. Many of the subjects in which it seemed likely Colonial Williamsburg would be most interested--the actual number of slaves in Williamsburg, the distribution of ownership, the work the slaves performed, their living conditions--were precisely the features of slavery most likely to be modified by whatever urban characteristics Williamsburg possessed.

Certain other parts of the report, which touch matters of criminal law, runaways, religion, and education apply much more generally to town and plantation alike. Even here, however, I have tried to come as quickly as possible to their specific relevance to Williamsburg.

There are no doubt some omissions that may have arisen from this attempt to limit the scope of the report as far as possible to Williamsburg, and there is almost certainly much about plantation slave life that could have been useful in the interpretation of the eighteenth century that Colonial Williamsburg undertakes. However, a detailed investigation of plantation slavery in colonial Virginia, one that would really present new information, would constitute a project of major proportions without necessarily meeting the immediate need of specific information on Williamsburg. It might also, I think, increase rather than diminish the problem of the shortage of sources of information on an inarticulate part of the population.

Thanks to the excellent working collection of the Colonial Williamsburg Research Library, especially its holdings of microfilmed documents from many English and

American depositories, I have had the novel experience of being able to complete this study largely in that library. The references in the bibliography will make it apparent, however, that I am indebted to a number of other libraries, whose librarians so willingly made parts of their collection available for microfilming and use by the staff of Colonial Williamsburg. I completed the original report, as the reader will infer from my earlier comments, while I was a member of the Colonial Williamsburg research staff myself, and I still carry many pleasant memories of the spirit of cooperation and stimulus to scholarship that prevailed among the community of fellow historians and other research staff members with whom I was then associated.

June, 1964   T. W. T.

XIII.

TABLE OF CONTENTS

The Negro
in Eighteenth-Century
Williamsburg

CHAPTER I

THE SEVENTEENTH CENTURY: THE EMERGENCE OF SLAVERY

Almost everyone who has even the slightest knowledge of the history of colonial Virginia inevitably recalls the year 1619 for three events. In addition to the first meeting of a representative assembly in the New World and the arrival of a shipload of marriageable maidens, the third occurrence was, of course, the landing of a cargo of Negroes in the James River, the first to be imported to the North American continent. The coming of these Negroes, twenty in all, was almost certainly accidental. They were aboard a Dutch frigate which touched Virginia in late August after a plundering expedition in West Indian waters. Arriving at Point Comfort, the Dutch captain struck a bargain with the Governor and the Cape Merchant to leave the twenty in exchange for sorely needed food. Not much later the Treasurer, a vessel fitted out in Virginia, left a single Negro in the colony. In all,

then, twenty-one Negroes came in that first eventful
year.[1]

Although scholars have in some cases been insisting on the opposite for better than a half century,
popular understanding has all too often continued to em-
brace some questionable assumptions about these first
Negroes. It has been all but impossible to correct the
impressions that slavery immediately became a precise,
legally defined institution; that the white colonists
just as quickly saw the Africans as a solution to the
pressing labor shortage of the colony; and that, as a
consequence, a rapidly swelling wave of slave labor began to flow into Virginia from 1619 on. Such viewpoints
deserve to be suspect for their insistent note of imme-
diacy, if nothing else. The processes of history normally move more slowly, and the emergence of slavery in

---

1. There are accounts of the landing of the first
Negroes in virtually every general account of seventeenth
century Virginia. Probably the most useful, because of
its superior documentation, is that in James Curtis Ballagh,
A History of Slavery in Virginia (Baltimore, 1902), pp. 7-9.
The pertinent sources include Susan Myra Kingsbury, (ed.),
The Records of the Virginia Company of London (Washington,
1906-1935), III, 243; Edward Arber, (ed.), Travels and
Works of Captain John Smith (Edinburgh, 1910), II, 541-542.

Virginia is no exception. Awareness of the economic use-fulness of slave labor, the importation of Negroes in quantity, and the legal recognition of slavery were not instantaneous consequences of what happened in the year 1619.

These first Negroes came into a society in which an unfree status, that of the indentured servant, was al-ready well known. Since the twenty on board the Dutch frig-ate were acquired by the Governor and the Cape Merchant in exchange for public stores, they presumably took their place alongside the other servants of the London Company.[2] Over the next four years these twenty, plus three or four others who were brought in on other ships, became scattered out to several of the settlements in the colony, where they were in the possession of some seven different men, most of whom were officers in the government.[3]

Thus was established a pattern of indentured ser-vitude for Negroes which continued until about mid-century.[4]

---

2. Records of Virginia Company, III, 243.

3. Ballagh, Slavery in Virginia, pp. 29-30.

4. The most comprehensive recent statement of the gradually emerging character of Negro slavery is Oscar and Mary F. Handlin, "Origins of the Southern Labor System,"

Like other servants the Negroes completed a period of service and became freemen. Some of them became land-owners and masters of other servants. One of the best known of these was Anthony Johnson, who had apparently reached Virginia in 1621 and had within a year or two gained his freedom. Johnson then married Mary, a Negro woman who came on the Margrett and John in 1622. He be-gan to acquire property and to import Negro servants of his own, until he had developed a small African community

---

William and Mary Quarterly, 3rd series, VII (April, 1950), 199-222. A briefer statement can be found in John Hope Franklin, From Slavery to Freedom: A History of American Negroes (New York, 1948), pp. 70-72. Ballagh, Slavery in Virginia, pp. 27-90, first established the slow develop-ment of slavery in a legal sense. John Henderson Russell, The Free Negro in Virginia, 1619-1865 (Baltimore, 1913), p. 23ff., also supports the evolution of Negro slavery from indentured servitude.

There are, however, some modern historians who chal-lenge this view and who regard slavery as having been the status of Negroes almost from the moment of their impor-tation into Virginia. This is true of Susie M. Ames, Studies of the Virginia Eastern Shore in the Seventeenth Century (Richmond, Va., 1940), pp. 100ff., and Wesley Frank Craven, The Southern Colonies in the Seventeenth Century, 1607-1689 (Baton Rouge, La., 1949), p. 402. Another recent statement of this view occurs in a paper given by Robert D. Ronsheim at the 1956 meeting of the Southern Historical Association and summarized in Journal of Southern History, XXIII (February, 1957), 79. Mr. Ronsheim viewed as more important, however, the rela-tionship of plantation size to labor force and the de-termination of when large plantations directly affected the labor system.

in Northampton County.[5] One of Anthony Johnson's former

Negro servants, Richard Johnson, a carpenter, was even

able to import two white servants for whom he received

the customary headrights of fifty acres.[6] There are a

number of other instances of Negroes who before 1660 ac-

quired land on headrights, by lease, or through purchase.[7]

The word "slave" does appear from time to time

before the 1660's, but there is no way to prove that it

had a meaning in law. Rather, it was a popular expres-

sion of the rigorous demands of servitude, applied to Ne-

gro and white alike, as in the case of the poor planters

who complained that their children were being held as

"slaues or drudges" for the debts of their parents.[8]

Gradually, however, in the period roughly be-

tween 1640 and 1660 the Negro's status in Virginia soci-

ety began to decline and white and Negro servants were

---

5. The Negro in Virginia. Compiled by the Writers'
Program of the Work Projects Administration (New York,
1940), pp. 11-12.

6. Ibid., p. 11.

7. Ibid.

8. For a fuller treatment of the colloquial usage
of the term slave, see Handlins, "Southern Labor System,"
pp. 203-204.

no longer approximate equals. In time the Negro found himself in lifetime bondage. The precise rate at which this subjection of the black man occurred as well as the reasons why it happened are subjects of dispute among historians. In large part the disagreement becomes one over whether slavery followed from racial prejudice or whether racial prejudice gripped whites only as a consequence of the enslavement of the Negro. Those who place the appearance of legalized slavery comparatively late, that is, no earlier than 1660, argue that the white colonists were originally without prejudice, developing it only when they came to know the Negro in bondage. On the other hand, those who believe that slavery developed more rapidly, existing in custom and recognized by the courts in individual instances at least by 1640, conclude that immediate antipathy toward the Negro served to bring on his decline. In truth, the argument focuses on a comparatively brief period--twenty years at the most--during which evidence of the legal recognition of slavery and of racial feeling appear more or less simultaneously. There seems to be little reason not to believe that the two factors, rather than presenting a distinct order of causality, might not have reacted upon each other, "dynamically joining hands to hustle the Negro down the road to complete degradation."[9]

In some part, then, slavery may have emerged not because of a desire to discriminate against the Negro but as the incidental result of increasing pressure to define length and conditions of service for white settlers. In the first years of the colony formal indentures were not the rule, and many persons spent long, indefinite periods as servants.[10] Eventually, in order to assure a continuing flow of indentured labor, it became necessary to write into law strict limitations on

---

9. Winthrop D. Jordan, "Modern Tensions and the Origins of American Slavery," Journal of Southern History, XXVIII (Feb., 1962), 29. This article, the most recent discussion of the subject, is the source of the conclusion stated above that slavery and prejudice were simultaneous developments. The principal contemporary spokesmen for the late development of slavery are the Handlins, "Southern Labor System," and Kenneth M. Stampp, The Peculiar Institution: Slavery in the Ante-Bellum South (New York, 1956), pp. vii-viii, 3-33. Carl N. Degler presents the case for early racial prejudice as a cause of slavery in "Slavery and the Genesis of American Race Prejudice," Comparative Studies in Society and History, II (Oct., 1959), 49-66, and also in his Out of the Past: The Forces that Shaped Modern America (New York, 1959), pp. 26-39. See also the works by Susie M. Ames and Wesley F. Craven, cited in note 4 above.

10. Handlins, "Southern Labor System," pp. 209-210.

servitude that held out the hope of life as a freeman and landowner. The initial statute in Virginia was one of 1642/43 fixing the limits of service for persons arriving without indentures at four years for those over the age of 20, five years for those from 12 to 20, and seven years for children under 12.[11] This law applied specifically to English servants, but subsequent modifications guaranteed a fixed term for all white Christians, no matter from where they came.[12]

The Negro servant, however, was another case. His coming was involuntary, and his bargaining power nonexistent. It became clearer and clearer to white masters that there was no reason for releasing a Negro servant in a few years and every advantage in claiming his labor indefinitely. Thus, in the same decades of the 1640's and 1650's in which the term of indenture for whites was becoming fixed and short, the Negro was coming to be regarded as a "servant for life."

---

11. William Waller Hening, (ed.), The Statutes at Large Being a Collection of all the Laws of Virginia (Richmond, Va., etc., 1810-1823), I, 257.

12. Ibid., I, 411, 441-442, 538-539; II, 113-114, 169, 297.

The life-time service of many Negroes was at first a matter of custom rather than law, but court decisions recognizing the principle were becoming more frequent. The earliest known case involved three runaway servants, one a Negro, who were recovered in Maryland and brought to trial in 1640. The two white men had their time of service extended by a year plus three years of labor on public works, but the Negro was ordered to serve for the balance of his life.[13] The fate of Manuel, a mulatto who had been bought "as a Slave for Ever" in September, 1644, and then was adjudged not to be a slave and freed in 1665, was an exception; but it indicates the prevailing trend.[14] Another example concerns the same Anthony Johnson who had established on the Eastern Shore a colony of Negroes indentured to him. In 1653 Johnson was involved

---

13. Helen T. Catterall, (ed.), Judicial Cases Concerning American Slavery and the Negro (Washington, 1924-1926), I, 77. E. Franklin Frazier, The Negro in the United States (New York, 1949), pp. 23-24. Philip Alexander Bruce, Economic History of Virginia in the Seventeenth Century (New York, 1895-1907), II, 23.

14. Catterall, Judicial Cases, I, 58-59; Negro in Virginia, pp. 13-14; "Randolph Manuscript," Virginia Magazine of History and Biography, XVII (July, 1909), 232.

in a suit brought by one of his men, John Casor, over the length of time for which Casor was obligated. Johnson succeeded in making good his claim to the man's service for life.[15]

The first recognition in statutory law of this state of affairs occurred in March, 1660/61. At that, this law was no more than an oblique recognition that life servitude was now a possibility for some Negroes; for it was enacted to deal with English servants who might "run away in company with any negroes who are incapable of making satisfaction by addition of time."[16]

Besides the widening gap in the length of service demanded of white and Negro servants, a few other distinctions began to appear in these years to the disadvantage of the black man. These restrictions bear some of the marks of racial prejudice. Negroes were excluded, for instance, by a statute of January, 1639/40 from the

---

15. Negro in Virginia, pp. 11-12; Frazier, Negro in the United States, p. 25.

16. Hening, Statutes, II, 26. Any English servant found guilty under this act was to have time equal to the Negro's absence added to his term of servitude. The same law was re-enacted in the following March (1661/2). Hening, Statutes, II, 117.

requirement of possessing arms and ammunition.[17] Three

years later Negro women servants, but not white women

servants, were counted as tithables for purposes of tax-

ation.[18] And in 1641 the outcome of a suit brought by a

Negro servant to confirm his ownership of some hogs sug-

gested that Negroes, even when indentured for a fixed

time, were more closely restricted than whites in their

right to possess personal property.[19]

Once the law of 1660/61 had admitted the possi-

bility of life servitude, there followed a period lasting

down to about 1675 or 1680 during which a number of laws

confirmed or defined further the Negro's lower status.

More and more, these differentiations cut the Negro "apart

from all other servants and gave a new depth to his bond-

age."[20] By 1670, for instance, the laws of the colony

---

17. Hening, Statutes, I, 226.

18. Ibid.,I, 242. Bruce, Economic History of Virginia, II, 101-102, regards this as not a matter of racial discrim- ination but a reflection of the use of Negro women largely as field hands and also of the desire not to discourage in any way the emigration of white women servants. Nonetheless, it served to set the Negro apart in some sense.

19. Catterall, Judicial Cases, I. 57-58.

20. Handlins, "Southern Labor System," p. 209.

clearly sought to make service for life the <u>normal</u> condition under which Negroes would in the future be introduced into Virginia.[21]

One step in this progressive decline of the
Negro's position was the elimination of Christianity as
a factor which might ameliorate his servitude. The seventeenth century was inclined to take seriously the proposition that conversion entitled heathen servants to liberty.[22] The fact was not lost on Virginians, however,
that a literal application of this principle could under-
mine the whole structure of perpetual servitude which had
so recently evolved. The General Assembly as early as
1667 eased the concern of owners of Negroes already in
the colony by decreeing that baptism "doth not alter the
condition of the person as to his bondage or ffreedome."[23]

Sealing off Christianity as a means of freedom
for Negroes yet to be imported could not be altered so
directly, however. There was still a reluctance to

---

21. Hening, <u>Statutes</u>, II, 283.

22. Ballagh, <u>Slavery in Virginia</u>, p. 46; Handlins,
"Southern Labor System," p. 212.

23. Hening, <u>Statutes</u>, II, 260.

legislate frankly along color lines, and the first attempt to insure life service for new Negroes drew the simple religious test of heathen and Christian on the assumption that most of the Negroes would certainly be unconverted. This occurred in the law of 1670 already cited in connection with life servitude. It stated that "all servants not being christians imported into this colony by shipping" were to be "slaves for their lives."[24] A certain number of Christianized Negroes escaped with short indentures under this enactment; but a 1682 law partially closed the loophole by denying eventual freedom to servants whose parentage and native country were not Christian and who were not themselves Christian at the time of their first purchase.[25] This was a test few of the new arrivals could meet. The 1705 act which codified much of the existing law on slaves and servants restated this formula a little more directly by declaring all servants imported into Virginia, except Turks and Moors, who were not Christian in their native country or

---

24. Hening, Statutes, II, 283.

25. Ibid., II, 491.

who were not free in a Christian country should be held
as slaves, regardless of any later conversion to Christianity.[26] In effect, then, Christianity ceased to shield
the newly imported Negro from slavery, just as it had not
after 1667 offered any hope of freedom to those who were
already here.

Another direct result of perpetual servitude
was an alteration in the methods of determining status
for Negro children. There had always been a problem
about the illegitimate offspring of all bound servants.
Now, however, the former legislation which depended prin-
cipally on additional terms of service--by the mother to
compensate her master for time lost during pregnancy and
by the father to compensate the parish for care of the
child--could no longer apply to most Negro parents.[27]
Where both parents were Negroes serving for life, the
necessity for punishment, as a matter of fact, ceased to
exist. By custom children born of such a union assumed
the status of the parents and became permanent and, in

---

26. Hening, Statutes, III, 447-448.

27. Ibid., I, 438; II, 114, 168; III, 139.

time, welcome additions to their owner's labor force.
If only one parent were a Negro, however, determination
of the child's status became more complicated. Here Virginia early arrived at the solution that children born in
the colony should "be held bond or free only according to
the condition of the mother."[28] An illegitimate offspring
of a mulatto mother, on the other hand, served as an indentured laborer and eventually became free.[29]

Whatever may have been the custom of the day,
the law continued during these years to regard the Negro's personal rights as substantially those of any other
servant. Statutory law sometimes employed the word slave,
but nearly always so that it read clearly in the context
of servant for life.[30] It is arguable that the distinction between being a servant for life and a chattel slave
was of no practical advantage; yet there was a difference. For one thing, there was less difficulty about the

---

28. Hening, Statutes, II, 170. This was enacted
in 1662.

29. Ibid., IV, 133.

30. Ibid., II, 260, 283, 299, 491. In particular,
the 1670 law speaks of "slaves for their lives" and that
of 1672, of "any negroe, molatto, Indian slave, or servant for life."

possibility of gaining freedom.[31] Also, the courts were
more inclined to deal with a servant, even one bound per-
petually, as a man rather than as a species of property.

During the last quarter of the century, however,
the status of the Negro in the eyes of the law began to
change once more. His personal rights were reduced to a
minimum and he was left as a true chattel slave.[32] Thus,
it was comparatively late in the seventeenth century before slavery became fixed in the form in which we know it
in the eighteenth and nineteenth centuries.

Now there appeared rudimentary "black codes,"
the first of the laws controlling the conduct, freedom of
movement, and personal rights of Negroes that were to become so common a feature of slavery. A 1680 statute,
ostensibly enacted to prevent insurrection but in actual
practice designed to curb freedom of movement and resistance to a white man, marked the effective beginning of

---

31. Bruce, Economic History of Virginia, II, 124.

32. The 1669 law (Hening, Statutes, II, 270) providing that the killing of a Negro under correction was not a
felony is a somewhat earlier example of a loss of an important legal protection by the Negro. However, the reasoning of the preamble was that a Negro could not serve additional time as a punishment, hence corporal punishment was
the only disciplinary force available, and that the master

these regulations. Subsequent laws soon established trial procedures which differed from those for white servants.[33]

Color now became the determining factor of slavery. Though there had undoubtedly been some racial antipathy toward Negroes almost from the beginning, the Virginians seemed in no hurry to write it into law.[34] The first law in which "Negro" was clearly used to show racial feeling rather than to distinguish two types of bound labor was perhaps the 1670 enactment forbidding free Negroes and Indians to own white servants.[35] The first act on Negro insurrections in 1680 carried the feeling a step further by punishing the black man who should "presume to lift up his hand in opposition against any christian," and the perpetual banishment after 1691 of any white who

---

might therefore have to be protected from the consequences of corporal punishment which killed a Negro. In that sense, the law was primarily a consequence of life-time servitude.

33. Hening, Statutes, II, 481-482, 492-493; III, 86-88, 102-103. The subject of colonial "black codes" is developed at greater length below, Chapter X, sec. 1.

34. Ibid., I, 146, 552; Handlins, "Southern Labor System," p. 216.

35. Hening, Statutes, I, 280-281.

married a Negro or mulatto more or less completed the circle.[36] Yet, as late as 1705, in defining slave status the law still clung to the elaborate fiction of heathen birth rather than color.[37] But by this time everyone must have known color was the real badge of slavery.

The last door of escape from a life-time of slavery was closed against the Negro in 1691, when owners were forbidden to free a slave except by transporting him from the colony within six months.[38] Except for a handful of slaves freed by special acts of the General Assembly the practical possibility of manumission had virtually ceased to exist.

From a legal point of view perhaps the final step in reducing a human to the level of slavery is to say point-blank that he has ceased to be a man and has become a species of property. In Virginia this was foreshadowed as early as 1669.[39] In 1705 the Assembly stated

---

36. Hening, Statutes, II, 481; III, 87.

37. Ibid., III, 447-448.

38. Ibid., III, 87-88.

39. By the law exempting masters from punishment for killing a slave under correction, it being presumed the owner would not willfully destroy his own estate. Ibid., II, 270. See also: II, 288.

explicitly that "all negro, mulatto, and Indian slaves, in all courts of judicature, and other places, within this dominion, shall be held, taken, and adjudged to be real estate..."[40] There was an attempt in 1748 to make slaves personal rather than real property, but it was part of a law which received the royal disallowance.[41] It was difficult to apply the principle that the slave was mere property in every case, however; and in practice both law and custom were forced from time to time to recognize the slave as a person.[42] But the fact remains that in becoming a slave the Negro had become a piece of property first and a man only secondarily.

If the development of slavery was such a slow process, requiring almost until the end of the seventeenth century to reach its final stage, then the assumption that the colonial planters immediately saw the Negro as an ideal answer to such problems as the chronic labor

40. Hening, Statutes, III, 333.

41. Ibid., V, 432-433.

42. Ballagh, Slavery in Virginia, pp. 96ff., though the case for the personal rights of the slave is considerably overstated.

shortage and the rigorous heat of the Southern climate becomes untenable.[43] In fact, the colonists continued for some time to prefer white labor, even with the disadvantage of short indentures. Much of the degradation in status of the Negro may have come about because the planters wanted white labor and set out to make the terms of indentured service more attractive. Lacking similar bargaining power, the Negro was more or less caught in the backwash.[44] Not even the extension of the headright system to Negroes in 1635 had any immediate effect on the number of Negroes imported, for only in the last ten years of the century did the patent books record any significant numbers of African headrights.[45]

---

43. For an expression of this older, deterministic view see Bruce, Economic History of Virginia, II, 57ff. It is also an important theme in the work of Ulrich B. Phillips.

44. Handlins, "Southern Labor System," pp. 206-208; Stampp, The Peculiar Institution, pp. 1-3; Craven, Southern Colonies in the Seventeenth Century, pp. 25, 214-215.

45. Negro in Virginia, p. 4; Bruce, Economic History of Virginia, II, 85; William and Mary Quarterly, 1st ser., VII (April, 1899), 281-287.

It is also absolutely fundamental to any understanding of this formative period to remember how small
the Negro population of Virginia actually was before 1680
or 1690. It may be more than coincidence that the appearance of true slavery and the beginning of a sizeable in-
flux of Negroes into Virginia coincide so closely. From
the first arrival to the beginning of the last quarter of
the century there was never more than an occasional importation of Negroes. The census of 1624-1625 counted
only 23. In 1648 an estimate listed 300 "Negro servants"
as compared with 15,000 white settlers, the Negroes being
no more than 2% of the colony's total population. By
Governor Berkeley's estimate in 1671, Negroes comprised
about 4% of the total, or 2,000 out of a population of
48,000.[46]

Over the decade of the 1670's the black population rose another thousand to 3,000.[47] By 1700 there were

---

46. All the above figures are collected in Evarts B.
Greene and Virginia D. Harrington, American Population Before the Federal Census of 1790 (New York, 1932), p. 136.

47. Ibid., p. 137.

about 16,390 Negro inhabitants of Virginia.[48] Thus, the closing thirty years of the seventeenth century saw a small, but significant, step-up in the arrival of Negroes; but the mass importations belong to the eighteenth century.

As the new century opened, there was no doubt that slavery had become a fixed, legally defined institution in the colony of Virginia. The use of Negro labor was moreover finding wider acceptance, and larger importations of slaves were beginning to occur. The way stood open for the enormous extension of slavery which occurred in the first half of the eighteenth century.

---

48. The latest estimates of Negro population are in U. S. Bureau of the Census, Historical Statistics of the United States: Colonial Times to 1957 (Washington, 1960), p. 756. With figures of 9,345 in 1690 and 16,390 in 1700 these estimates are larger than many previous ones for these two decades, but they agree with the older figures for all the earlier decades.

Chapter II

THE EIGHTEENTH CENTURY: THE GROWTH OF SLAVERY

The 16,390 Negroes residing in Virginia in 1700 had grown to 26,559 by 1720, to 30,000 by 1730, or almost double the 1700 figure. In the next decade--the 1730's-- the Negro population doubled once again, reaching an estimated 60,000.[1] It was not long until annual importations of Negroes had climbed to a peak of three or four thousand a year, while the number of Virginia-born Negroes increased correspondingly.[2]

By mid-century the estimates of population varied widely, but Governor Dinwiddie's 1756 figures were perhaps as reliable as any. Estimating from the count of tithables,

---

1. U. S. Bureau of the Census, Historical Statistics of the United States: Colonial Times to 1957 (Washington, 1960), p. 756; Evarts B. Greene and Virginia D. Harrington, American Population Before the Federal Census of 1790 (New York, 1932), p. 139; Lawrence H. Gipson, The British Empire before the American Revolution (Caldwell, Idaho, and New York, 1936-   ), II, 107.

2. Lewis Cecil Gray, History of Agriculture in the Southern United States to 1860 (New York, 1941), I, 355.

he arrived at a total population in Virginia of 293,472,
of which 173,316 were white and 120,156 Negro. By the
1760's the proportion of white to Negro was not quite
half and half, a ratio which remained more or less constant to the end of the eighteenth century. As was to
be expected, the highest density of Negroes occurred in
the Tidewater, but slaves were also numerous in the
Piedmont. Only in the Valley and in the mountain areas
was the Negro population really small.[3]

This rapid increase did not depend alone on
the willingness of the colonial planters to employ Negro
labor. It also demanded the evolution of an efficient,
large-scale slave trade.[4] Through much of the seventeenth century sporadic Dutch trading activity was

---

3. Greene and Harrington, American Population,
pp. 139-143. Historical Abstracts of the United States,
p. 756.

4. This discussion is no more than a very general
and tentative summary of a phase of slavery in colonial
Virginia that needs extensive re-study. In particular,
there is a need to relate the slave trade to the rest of
the Virginia economy and to analyze the attempts of the
Virginia Assembly to block or discourage the overseas
slave trade by import duties.
Many of the most important documents are assembled
in Elizabeth Donnan, (ed.), Documents Illustrative of the
History of the Slave Trade to America (Washington, 1935),
IV, 2-7, 49-234.

responsible for most of the importations of Negroes.[5]
The Virginia Assembly attempted to encourage this trade
in 1659 by exempting Dutch merchants from paying ten
shillings per hogshead duty on tobacco received for
Negroes, permitting them to pay instead the two shillings
English duty.[6]

English mercantile interests did not become
actively involved in the African slave trade until the
Restoration. In 1662 The Company of Royal Adventurers
Trading to Africa received a monopoly of the slave trade.
This company, however, survived for only ten difficult
years and never recorded a contract for supplying Virginia with Negroes.[7] In 1672 a new company, the Royal
African Company, received a charter which passed along
to it the monopoly of the slave trade to the English colonies. There has been a tendency to assume too easily

---

5. Gray, *Agriculture in the Southern United States*,
I, 353.

6. William Waller Hening, (ed.), *The Statutes at
Large Being a Collection of all the Laws of Virginia*
(Richmond, Va., etc., 1810-1823), I, 540.

7. Gray, *Agriculture in the Southern United States*,
I, 352.

that the company was able to take full advantage of its favored position.[8] In reality, the Royal African Company found it difficult to protect itself against interlopers from both England and the colonies. Not even the support of the Crown, which consistently instructed royal governors to give all possible encouragement to the company, could help.[9] The Royal African Company contracted on several occasions in the 1670's for shipments of Negroes to Virginia and made some deliveries.[10] But, even though Governor Culpeper's statement that the company had never sold slaves in the colony was obviously an exaggeration, the Royal African Company was unsuccessful in dominating the Virginia market.[11]

Some of the challengers of the company monopoly seemed to have established good local connections in

---

8. James Curtis Ballagh, A History of Slavery in Virginia (Baltimore, 1902), p. 10; Philip Alexander Bruce, Economic History of Virginia in the Seventeenth Century (New York, 1895-1907), II, 78, 82.

9. Donnan, (ed.), Documents, IV, 5, 55-56.

10. Ibid., IV, 53-55; Ballagh, Slavery in Virginia, p. 13.

11. Donnan, (ed.), Documents, IV, 5-6, 58.

Virginia through men like the first William Byrd and
William Fitzhugh. In the 1680's Byrd was interested in
a number of transactions that involved bringing in small
shipments of Negroes from the West Indies.[12] About the
same time Fitzhugh was in correspondence with a New
England merchant about the details of trading tobacco
for slaves.[13]

Ultimately, in 1698, the Royal African Company
lost its monopoly, being forced to give way to an arrangement which permitted "separate traders" to carry slaves
by paying certain duties to the company.[14] Other merchants
could now openly compete, sending their vessels, among
other places, to the landings and ports which dotted the
Virginia rivers. The figures for 1699-1708, which show
that the separate traders carried 5,692 Negroes to Virginia and the Royal African Company 679, are a clear

---

12. "Letters of William Byrd, First," Virginia
Magazine of History and Biography, XXIV (1916), 229, 232;
XXV (1917), 50, 52, 133.

13. "Letters of William Fitzhugh," Virginia Magazine,
I (October, 1893), 108.

14. Gray, Agriculture in the Southern United States,
I, 353.

indication of the weak position of the Company in the trade.[15] After these years shipments of slaves by the Company became increasingly intermittent, though there were still a few to Virginia in the 1720's.[16] Then, after 1730, it no longer shipped Negroes from the African coast.[17] The flow of slaves continued, however, with Bristol and Liverpool merchants dominating the trade. A sprinkling of New England vessels also brought slave cargoes from Africa, and a number of Virginia ships were employed to bring small groups of Negroes from the West Indies into the colony.[18]

As the century progressed, new Negroes were sold farther and farther up the rivers, until settlements on the Fall Line like Rocky Ridge, across the James from Richmond, became the most important slave markets in the colony. There was also a domestic trade in Virginia-born

15. Donnan, (ed.), Documents, IV, 172-173.

16. Ibid., IV, 184-185.

17. Gray, Agriculture in the Southern United States, I, 353-354.

18. Donnan, (ed.), Documents, IV, 188-234, passim.

Negroes, prized for their greater skill and adjustment
to white civilization and therefore commanding higher
prices.[19]

    As much as they had come to value slave labor,
Virginians viewed these large-scale importations of Negroes with misgivings.[20] No one has yet managed a completely satisfactory explanation of why the colonists
began to wish they could put some limit on the number of
slaves to be introduced into the colony. An older gen-
eration of Virginia historians claimed to find evidence
of moral and humanitarian objections to the trade in human beings.[21] Some of them have even charged that slaves
were forced on the Southern colonies by the pressure of
greedy British and New England mercantile groups.[22] Any
close reading of the evidence quickly suggests how little

---

19. Marcus W. Jernegan, Laboring and Dependent Classes
in Colonial America, 1607-1783 (Chicago, 1931), pp. 8-9.

20. John Hope Franklin, From Slavery to Freedom: A
History of American Negroes (New York, 1948), p. 72;
Ballagh, Slavery in Virginia, p. 11.

21. Ballagh, Slavery in Virginia, p. 11.

22. This was a favorite theme, for example, of Lyon G.
Tyler and one which he could contrive to inject into a discussion of virtually any subject.

support there is for this point of view, whether it be
the prevailing attitudes of most of the planters toward
the Negro or in the fact that no cargo of healthy slaves
ever lacked for purchasers. It is clear that much less
idealistic reasons were responsible for the planters' objections.

For one thing, social control of the Negro
played a large part in the increasing uneasiness of the
whites. Fear of slave insurrection became a daily fact
of life in Virginia, and ultimately the slave owners came
to feel that there must be a limit beyond which the proportion of Negroes in the population could not safely go.
An economic factor was also involved. Often the explanation has been that owners of Negroes already in Virginia
had a speculative interest in keeping additional African
Negroes out in order to assure a steady increase in the
value of their own human property. What seems more convincing, however, is the fact that many planters opposed
the further drain of money and increase in colonial in-
debtedness that the purchase of African slaves necessarily
imposed. Prosperity in the slave trade was directly related to economic conditions of the tobacco market with
the result that it suffered some of the same consequences

of overextended credit. The more perceptive colonists were fully aware of the connection.[23]

The principal strategem which the leaders of the colony evolved for discouraging too rapid an increase in the number of slaves was an import duty on African slaves that could be disguised as a revenue measure.[24] The long series of laws which enacted these duties began as early as 1699, and, for the first few years, were honestly intended to raise funds rather than discourage trade. The initial act, for example, levied a charge of twenty shillings for each Negro imported specifically for the construction of the new Capitol at Williamsburg.[25] With one renewal this duty continued in force until late 1703.[26] After a three month interval in early 1704 during which no duty was in effect, the impost was revived in April,

---

23. Jerman Baker to Duncan Rose, February 15, 1764, in William and Mary Quarterly, 1st ser., XII (April, 1904), 242; Franklin, From Slavery to Freedom, pp. 72-73; Gray, Agriculture in the Southern United States, I, 356.

24. Gray, Agriculture in the Southern United States, I, 356-357; Ballagh, Slavery in Virginia, pp. 11-24; Donnan, (ed.), Documents, IV, 7.

25. Hening, Statutes, III, 193.

26. Ibid., III, 212-213.

1704.[27] From then until 1718 some form of duty was in
force without an important break. The tendency to make
the duties prohibitory in character also began to appear,
for during these years the amount climbed as high as £5
per Negro.[28]

From 1718 to 1723 the Assembly made no attempt
to continue the duty.[29] Then, in 1723 an attempt to re-
store it at the rate of 40 shillings touched off the
first organized opposition from English traders. The
flood of petitions and representations by these men
carried enough political weight to persuade the King to
disallow the 1723 law and all subsequent attempts of the
Assembly to pass a duty over the next nine years.[30]

By a change of tactics that made a 5% ad valorem
duty payable by the prospective buyer rather than by the
importer the General Assembly broke the deadlock in 1732.[31]

---

27. Hening, Statutes, III, 225, 229-235.

28. Ibid., III, 482; IV, 30; Ballagh, Slavery in Virginia, p. 15n.

29. Ballagh, Slavery in Virginia, p. 16.

30. Donnan, (ed.), Documents, IV, 102-127; Ballagh, Slavery in Virginia, pp. 16-17; Hening, Statutes, IV, 118.

31. Hening, Statutes, IV, 317-322.

Thereafter and until the outbreak of the Revolution an
ad valorem duty on slaves was in effect in Virginia, except for six months during 1751. The 5% rate of 1732 was
gradually increased, until it stood at 20% during part of
the French and Indian War. The whole effort to discourage the foreign slave trade led ultimately to the unsuccessful petition of the Assembly in 1772 for a complete
end to further importations and to the successful prohibition of the trade by the new state government in 1778.[32]
But these events are more logically a part of the American
Revolution in Virginia. Down to the outbreak of that
struggle African slavers and West Indian traders continued to land their human cargoes in the colony with but
little discouragement.

The role which the African Negroes and their
American-born descendants assumed in plantation society
possesses a certain familiarity. The fact that most his-
tories of slavery leap so quickly to the nineteenth century, where the details of plantation life survive so much

---

32. Ballagh, Slavery in Virginia, pp. 19-23; Hening, Statutes, IV, 394, 471-473; V, 28-31, 91-92, 160-161, 318-319; VI, 217-221, 353-354, 419, 466; VII, 81, 281, 363, 383, 639-642; VIII, 190-192, 237-238, 336-338, 530-532.

more abundantly, does place difficulties in the way of
a full picture of the eighteenth. However, the general
outlines of the work of the Negro slaves, of their daily
existence, and of their immovable position at the bottom
of a stratified colonial society seem clear enough.

The largest proportion of Negroes--men, women,
and children--were field hands, assigned to growing tobacco and the other marketable crops the colony produced.[33]
This was the real purpose for which slavery had evolved,
and it represented the institution in its most impersonal,
burdensome, and typical form. The account of the field
slave's lot by J. F. D. Smyth, an English traveller in
Virginia just before the Revolution, is admittedly an
unflattering one and no more to be accepted uncritically
than any other single observation; but it is probably
accurate enough in its description of the working day:

> ...He [the slave] is called up in the morn-
> ing at day break, and is seldom allowed time
> enough to swallow three mouthfuls of homminy,
> or hoecake, but is driven out immediately to
> the field to hard labour, at which he continues,
> without intermission, until noon....About noon

---

33. The Negro in Virginia. Compiled by the Writers'
Program of the Work Projects Administration (New York,
1940), pp. 58-66, is a satisfactory summary, though with
the usual heavy emphasis on the nineteenth century.

is the time he eats his dinner, and he is
seldom allowed an hour for that purpose....
    They [i.e., the slaves] then return to
severe labour, which continues in the field
until dusk in the evening, when they repair
to the tobaccohouses, where each has his
task in stripping alotted him, that employs
him for some hours.[34]

A smaller, but still significant number, of

slaves fared somewhat better as household workers and per-

sonal servants of the master's family.[35] Almost invar-

iably accounts of slaves who enjoyed especially lenient

treatment or some bond of affection from their masters

refer to Negroes from the household staff. Even so, there

has been an easy tendency to view this group of slaves in

a romantic light, and there is much we really do not know

about their life.

A third segment of the slave labor force was

composed of skilled and semi-skilled craftsmen. In time

Negroes performed substantially all of the work on

plantations in certain trades, especially carpentry and

---

34. "Smyth's Travels in Virginia, in 1773," Virginia
Historical Register, VI (April, 1853), 84-85. Smyth's description of the Negroes at work in the evening stripping
tobacco would obviously apply only at harvest.

35. Negro in Virginia, pp. 35-46, is a general account which leans heavily on a few well-known masters
like Jefferson, Wythe, and John Randolph.

cooperage.[36] Frequently, they were also proficient millers, tanners, shoemakers, wheelwrights, spinners, and weavers.[37] Not only did these slave artisans perform tasks necessary for individual plantations; they were also instrumental in the commercial development of the Southern colonies, especially in tanning, in the rudimentary iron industry which was developing, and in the preparation of lumber and staves for export.[38]

There are not many extant lists of slaves which provide a specific breakdown of the division of labor on the plantation from which they came. There is one, however, for Green Spring Plantation in 1770, when the estate of its deceased owner, Philip Ludwell, was being settled. At that time Ludwell's son-in-law, William Lee, described the slaves at Green Spring as including 59 "crop Negroes," a figure which was "exclusive of boys";

---

36. Jernegan, Laboring and Dependent Classes, pp. 9-12.

37. Ibid., pp. 10-12; Virginia Gazette (Purdie and Dixon), July 22, 1773; Hening, Statutes, III, 403-404.

38. Virginia Gazette (Purdie and Dixon), October 31, 1777; Jernegan, Laboring and Dependent Classes, pp. 22-23.

12 house servants; 4 carpenters; 1 wheelwright; 2 shoemakers; and 3 gardeners and hostlers.[39]

It is easy to overestimate the number of slaves
owned by an individual planter and even easier to mis-
calculate the number used to operate a single plantation
or quarter. The eighty-odd Negroes at Green Spring were
the largest single group from a combined total of 164 on
all the lands belonging to Philip Ludwell's estate.[40]
This total was more than enough to mark Ludwell as one of
the more substantial members of the planter aristocracy,
as his membership on the Governor's Council also testified.

If we were to judge Ludwell by the pattern of
slave ownership revealed in the tax records of the 1780's,
he would belong very nearly at the middle of the hundred
leading families of the colony. These tax records, which
have been most effectively analyzed by Professor Jackson T.
Main, furnish the only comprehensive records on how widely
slave ownership was distributed in Virginia before the

---

39. "Some Notes on 'Green Spring,'" Virginia Magazine,
XXXVII (October, 1929), 294.

40. Ibid., 293.

nineteenth century.[41] While the position of the leading families had begun to decline somewhat by the 1780's, the change was as yet so slight that the statistics are generally reliable for the entire later colonial period.[42]

What becomes immediately clear from these tax records is the error of regarding even most of the wealthiest planters as having owned "hundreds" of Negroes. One man, Charles Carter, owned 785. He was followed in turn by William Allen with 700, Robert Beverley of Essex County with 592, Robert Carter of Nomini Hall with 445, and David Ross, the Richmond merchant-planter, with 400. Aside from these top five there were only eighteen other men in the entire colony who owned more than 200 slaves. The average for the hundred leading families was about 180 slaves, eighty on the home plantation and about a hundred elsewhere. A number of families who fell within this top group owned far less than a hundred Negroes.

---

41. Jackson T. Main, "The One Hundred," William and Mary Quarterly, 3rd ser., XI (July, 1954), 354-384. Ulrich B. Phillips also used some of these records in American Negro Slavery (New York, 1918), pp. 83-84.

42. Main, "One Hundred," pp. 366-367.

If there were relatively few large-scale slave-holders in Virginia, the vast majority of families in the average Tidewater or Piedmont county nonetheless owned at least a small number of Negroes. In a sampling of eight of these counties the records indicated that three-fourths of the heads of families held slaves. Forty per cent of them, however, owned fewer than five Negroes.[43] In the light of these statistics a true picture of slavery in colonial Virginia must take into account the humbler man who owned no more than two or three slaves as well as the more substantial planter.

Until the rationale of the American Revolution had begun to work its logic on the minds of Virginians, any doubt which the average colonist ever had about the wisdom of slavery stemmed either from the unpleasant prospect that the slaves would one day rise up and butcher the master class or else from suspicion that, as a business proposition, slavery simply did not pay its way.[44] The threat of insurrection was in part dealt with through

---

43. Phillips, American Negro Slavery, pp. 83-84.

44. The question of possible moral and humanitarian objections to slavery is treated below, pp. 209-217, 222-233.

the tightening of the black codes, as well as by the attempt to discourage new importations of Negroes; but it
was less easy to deal so directly with the economics of
slavery.

The relative advantages and disadvantages of
slave labor was, however, a subject often on the mind of
the planter. Philip Fithian's account of a conversation
with the wife of Robert Carter adequately sums up the reaction in theory of many planters to a situation with
which they were unable to deal in fact:

> After Supper I had a long conversation
> with Mrs Carter concerning Negroes in Vir-
> ginia, & find that She esteems their value
> at no higher rate than I do. We both con-
> cluded, (& I am pretty certain that the
> conclusion is just) that if in Mr Carters,
> or in any Gentleman Estate, all the Negroes
> should be sold, & the Money put to Interest
> in safe hands, & let the Lands which these
> Negroes now work lie wholly uncultivated,
> the bare Interest of the Price of the
> Negroes would be a much greater yearly in-
> come than what is now received from their
> working the Lands, making no allowance at
> all for the trouble & Risk of the Masters
> as to the Crops, & Negroes.--How much
> greater then must be the value of an Es-
> tate here if these poor enslaved Africans
> were all in their native desired Country,
> & in their Room industrious Tenants, who
> being born in freedom, by a laudable care,
> would not onlyly inrich their Landlords,

but would raise a hardy Offspring to be the
Strength & honour of the Colony.[45]

One reason the planters questioned the profit in slave

labor was the high cost of investment in slaves. In more

pessimistic moments they also criticized their Negroes as

wasteful and unproductive workers, either from lack of

skill or deliberate resistance to forced labor.[46]

To a large degree, the planters were inclined

to rationalize other deficiencies in the agricultural

methods of the colony at the expense of their Negroes.

If there was one way in which slavery succeeded, it was

as an economic system. Any problems of debt or credit

arising from large investment in slaves was in reality

a by-product of the uncertainties of tobacco cultivation.

The supposed inefficiency and ineptitude of slave labor

was more likely to be the fault of the wasteful methods

---

45. Hunter Dickinson Farish, (ed.), Journals and
Letters of Philip Vickers Fithian, 1773-1774: A Plantation
Tutor of the Old Dominion (Williamsburg, Va., 1943),
p. 123.

46. "Diary of Col. Landon Carter," William and Mary
Quarterly, 1st ser., XIII (April, 1905), 223; John Spencer
Bassett, (ed.), The Writings of "Colonel William Byrd of
Westover in Virginia Esqr" (New York, 1901), pp. 347-348.

of farming common to almost everyone who tilled the
Virginia soil. Moreover, the cheapness of a slave's
maintenance easily outweighed high purchase price, lack
of training or skill, and even the prospect of his unproductive old age.[47]

Whatever doubts the Virginia planter may have
felt about the wisdom of enslaving an alien people, it
must have seemed in the mid-eighteenth century that slavery was certainly here to stay. The rapid growth of the
Negro population, the size of the slaveowners' investment, the usefulness of the labor, and outright fear
combined to make the replacement of slavery unthinkable.

---

47. The most satisfactory discussion of the economic
advantages of slavery is Gray, Agriculture in the Southern
United States, I, 368-371, 462-480.

Chapter III

THE NEGRO IN WILLIAMSBURG: AN INTRODUCTION

For an institution like slavery, which had developed in the first instance out of the needs of an agricultural society, urban life was bound to present something of an anomaly. We know, of course, from the rise of a few sizeable cities in the ante-bellum South that slavery resolved the contradictions involved with ease. Clearly, however, the use of slaves in a town environment necessitated modifications, if for no other reason than the fact that the largest single element in the slave labor force, the field hands, could have no part in urban slavery. These adjustments were apt to be small in eighteenth-century Virginia, where better than nine-tenths of the population still lived on farms and plantations. But a few towns, Williamsburg among them, had begun to develop as centers of commerce or government.

From the time of its founding Williamsburg was to be linked in many ways with the institution of Negro slavery. The first duty levied by the Assembly against imported Negroes had been intended to furnish money for building the Capitol. And when that construction began one of the first outlays had been £120 to purchase four Negro men "to labor in the business of the capital."[1] Nor should it be forgotten that the founding of Williamsburg came at a time when the institution of slavery had only recently begun to take hardened form in Virginia. Negroes in the colony had been significant in number for barely ten years. True slavery had not existed much longer. The planter class had just begun to appreciate the slaves as a valuable addition to the labor supply of the colony. Williamsburg's development, in short, was to coincide roughly with the real growth of Virginia slavery.

In a number of ways the story of Williamsburg's Negroes is that of the black population everywhere in the colony. The same laws governed them; the same efforts to

---

1. _William and Mary Quarterly_, 1st ser., XII (October, 1901), 82.

evangelize them, by turns fervent and lackadaisical,
prevailed; and ultimately the struggle for American independence was to affect them all alike. However, the
modifying influence of town life--not only in the different division of labor but also in the relative cosmopol-
itanism of Williamsburg--had its effect. It was against
this background that the Negroes of eighteenth-century
Williamsburg lived, providing a minor, but nonetheless
important, variant on the general history of slavery in
Virginia.

Chapter IV

PATTERNS OF SLAVE POPULATION AND OWNERSHIP IN WILLIAMSBURG

The first accurate count of the Negro population
of Williamsburg occurs no earlier than in the same tax records of the 1780's that provide the first comprehensive
record of the number and distribution of Negroes in all of
Virginia. The Williamsburg figures begin with a listing
of heads of families in 1782, also used to compute the
1790 United States Census returns for the town. They record a white population of 722 and a Negro population of
702.[1] Over the next few years the total figure for Negroes
stayed close to this one, 642 in 1783, 664 in 1784, and
689 in 1786.[2] A few free Negroes counted in 1782 and apparently not added to the later figures account for the

---

1. Evarts B. Greene and Virginia D. Harrington,
American Population Before the Federal Census of 1790
(New York, 1932), p. 153.

2. Williamsburg City. Personal Property Taxes,
1781-1861. Virginia State Library. (Colonial Williamsburg Microfilm.)

small decline. Thus, during the years immediately following the Revolution, the total Negro population remained at about 700. The 50-50 ratio between blacks and
whites also continued stable.

After 1786 the tax returns for Williamsburg no
longer listed all Negroes but only those 12 years of age
or older. Without the younger children it is impossible
to determine exactly the total population figure beyond
this date; however, we can compare the number of tithable
slaves, those over 16, in 1783 with the tithables between
1786 and the end of the century. There were in 1783 a
total of 350 tithable Negroes. After 1786 the figure was
not much different, ranging between 325 and 353.[3] There
is, as a matter of fact, so little variation in the count
of tithables that the total Negro population must also
have remained very stable. In other words, the Negro population of Williamsburg probably stayed at around 700
throughout the last two decades of the century.

Estimating the number of Negroes living in
Williamsburg before the Revolution is another matter.

---

3. Williamsburg City. Personal Property Taxes, 1786-
1800. Virginia State Library. (Colonial Williamsburg Microfilm.)

There are no tax returns to show either exact population or the ratio of Negroes and whites. The only possible comparison is between a single set of returns of tithables in 1755 and those of 1782-1783.[4] Williamsburg was not listed separately in the 1755 count, however, making it necessary to work with the combined total for James City and York Counties and Williamsburg:

Table No. 1

A Comparison of Tithables in 1755
and 1782-1783

Tithables, 1755

	White	Negro	Total	%Negro
James City	394	1254	1648	
York	562	1567	2129	
Williamsburg	(Included in above figures)			
	956	2821	3777	75%

Tithables, 1782-83

	White	Negro	Total	%Negro
James City	493	1832	2325	
York	699	2063	2762	
Williamsburg	126	350	476	
	1318	4245	5563	76% [5]

4. Both male and female Negroes above the age of 16 were counted as tithable, whereas in the white population only males above 21 were counted.

5. Greene and Harrington, American Population, pp. 150-153. The James City and York figures are for 1782 and the Williamsburg figures are for 1783.

Since Williamsburg cannot be isolated from the total figure, this comparison has its limitations. It at least
suggests, however, that the proportion of tithables who
were Negro remained about the same, roughly three-quarters.
If this ratio remained fixed, then it is not likely that
the approximately equal proportion of whites and Negroes
in the total population varied significantly either. At
any time after the middle of the eighteenth century, then,
the Negroes in Williamsburg probably constituted about
one-half the total resident population. In this respect
Williamsburg did not differ greatly from the rural areas
in Tidewater and Piedmont.

There were only a handful of free Negroes counted
in Williamsburg in 1782. The four free Negro families
listed comprised 11 persons in all, and in each case the
head of the family was a woman--Sally Carter, Nanny Jones,
Elizabeth Rozario, and Betty Wallace.[6] The voluntary
manumission law passed that same year; so the increase in
free Negroes resulting from that legislation had not yet
begun to occur. To judge from the smallness of the 1782

---

6. First Census of the United States, 1790: Records
of the State Enumerations: 1782-1785: Virginia (Washington,
1908).

figure, it is hardly likely that free Negroes were numerous or important in pre-Revolutionary Williamsburg.

Like the rest of Tidewater and Piedmont Virginia slaveholding appears to have been extremely wide-
spread in Williamsburg. Once again it is the tax and
census records for the immediate post-Revolutionary years
that provide the only systematic information about the
pattern of slave ownership. Most of the tabulations which
follow are drawn from that source.[7] At least five-sixths
of the families living here in the 1780's owned some
slaves, as the following table indicates:

Table No. 2

Slave Ownership by Williamsburg Families

Year	Number of Households	Number Own- ing Slaves	% Owning Slaves
1782	155	135	88%
1783	134	112	84%
1784	112	98	88%

When the number of families owning slaves is
compared with the slave population for the same years,
the average holding of an individual family or household

---

7. Williamsburg City, Personal Property Taxes; First
Census of United States, Virginia Heads of Families.

works out to five or six Negroes--4.5 per family in 1782,
4.8 in 1783, and 5.9 in 1784. This average figure is not
of much value in the sense of enabling one to say that
the "typical" Williamsburg family owned exactly 4 or 5
slaves. It is, however, a good indication that extremely
large numbers of slaves in a single household were excep-
tional. There is, however, some indication that this
average was increasing, a point which can be amplified
from Table No. 3:

Table No. 3

Size of Slave Holdings of Williamsburg Families

No. of Slaves Owned	Number of Families			Percentage of Families		
	1782	1783	1784	1782	1783	1784
1-2	52	35	20	38.5%	31.2%	20.4%
3-5	38	32	31	28.0%	28.6%	31.6%
6-9	27	27	23	20.0%	21.4%	23.5%
10-19	16	16	22	12.0%	17.9%	22.4%
20 or more	2	2	2	1.5%	0.9%	2.1%
	135	112	98			

Thus, in 1782 more than a third of Williamsburg's
slaveowners held no more than one or two Negroes. Then
over the next two years the percentage of small owners fell
rapidly. Their decline raises the question of whether some
of the lesser artisans, journeymen, and other more modest

citizens might not have been the first to feel any economic pinch caused by the removal of the capital to
Richmond. At any rate there are some 64 heads of families from the 1782 list who do not reappear on subsequent lists, and in almost every case they either owned
a small number of slaves or none at all.

Meanwhile the proportion of larger slaveowners
increased during these same years, and thereby the total
slave population in Williamsburg remained fairly stable.
However, the greater number of people continued to keep
no more than three to ten slaves; and there were only
about two dozen who had more than ten Negroes at any time
during this three-year period.

Table No. 4

Williamsburg Residents Owning Ten or More Slaves, 1782-1784.

Name	Number of Slaves Listed		
	1782	1783	1784
Robert Anderson	13	12	11
John Blair	18	17	17
Christiana Campbell	19	13	10
Robey Coke	10	2	--
Dudley Digges	--	14	16
James Galt	11	9	8
John Galt	9	10	10
John Greenhow	17	16	20
Corbin Griffin (Sam'l Griffin, 1784)	15	12	13
William Holt	23	21	--
Joseph Hornsby	--	17	10
David Hubard	12	13	--

Table No. 4 (contd.)

Williamsburg Residents Owning Ten or More Slaves, 1782-1784

Name	Number of Slaves Listed		
	1782	1783	1784
James Innes	--	9	14
William Lewis	8	8	10
Gabriel Maupin	17	19	17
Elizabeth Nelson	--	--	19
Thomas Nelson	6	--	44
Robert Nicolson	12	12	11
Joseph Prentis	9	11	12
Betty Randolph	15	--	--
George Reid	4	14	13
Mrs. Lewis Riddle	16	15	15
John Saunders	10	11	12
James Southall	21	19	17
Charles Taliaferro	11	13	7
Benjamin Waller	16	13	10
George Wythe	9	14	17

Random examples from the years before 1776 suggest that about the same number of slaves--no more than ten to twenty for even the most prominent citizens--sufficed then as well.[8] The 27 slaves in the inventory of Peyton Randolph's estate in 1776 were the largest number owned by any Williamsburg resident up to that date for which any records could be found.[9] Governor Fauquier owned 17 at his death and John Prentis, who had been mayor of Williamsburg, owned 15.[10]

---

8. See Table No. 5.

9. York County Records, Wills and Inventories, Book 22, pp. 337-341.

10. Ibid., Wills and Inventories, Book 22, pp. 91, 313-320.

There were many more instances of men who possessed a far

smaller number, lending some support to the supposition

that the post-Revolutionary figures for the percentage of

families owning slaves and for the average number of slaves

owned by a family were not much different before 1776.

Table No. 5

Examples of Numbers of Slaves Owned in Williamsburg
Before 1776

Owner	Year of Death	No. of Slaves in Estate	Ref. in York County Records
John Marot	1717	5	O & W, 15, 242-46
Orlando Jones	1719	10	", 529
David Cunningham	1719	7	", 562
Robert Davidson	1739	3	W & I, 18, 587-88
John Carter	1741	4	W & I, 19, 91-92
Thomas Pattison	1742	6	", 177-79
William Keith	?	8	", 282
John Burdett	1746	6	W & I, 20, 46-48
Ishmael Moody	1748	10	", 134-38
James Wray	1750	20	", 204-08
Mark Cosby	1752	5	", 277
Kenneth MacKenzie	1755	5	", 364-66
Henry Weatherburn	1760	13	W & I, 21, 43
John Coke	1768	9	", 381-84
Peter Hay	1769	11	", 444-48
William Waters	1769	6	", 463-66
Anthony Hay	1771	20	W & I, 22, 19-24
Francis Fauquier	1771	17	", 91ff.
Joseph Scrivener	1772	4	", 118-120
Thomas Cobb	1774	4	", 245-46
Matthew Tuell	1775	2	", 253-54
Matthew Moody	1775	4	", 296-97
John Prentis	1775	15	", 313-20
Alexander Craig	1776	8	", 330-37
Peyton Randolph	1776	27	", 337-41
Alexander Purdie	1779	13	", 437-42
Henry Bowcock	1779	5	", 447-48

In the final analysis four major conclusions stand out about the slave population and the pattern of slave ownership in Williamsburg during the immediate post-Revolutionary years. And, in a much more tentative way, they can also be applied to the more flourishing years before the removal of the seat of government. They are:

1. The number of Negroes and whites in the resident population of Williamsburg was approximately equal.

2. An overwhelming majority, roughly five-sixths, of the families in Williamsburg owned slaves.

3. A large percentage of these slaveowners were, nevertheless, persons of modest estate who might own no more than one or two slaves. After the Revolution, however, the proportion of small-scale owners was decreasing rapidly.

4. Even the wealthier men, innkeepers, etc., who were among the larger slaveowners in Williamsburg, normally kept only a moderate number of slaves, usually from about ten to fifteen and seldom more than twenty.

Chapter V

(THE WORK OF THE NEGRO IN WILLIAMSBURG)

To make too much of eighteenth-century Williamsburg as an urban economy may be inaccurate to a degree,
since the Virginia capital owed its creation and its continuing life so largely to the business of politics and
government. To a large extent the town represented a con-
centration of semi-agrarian households whose gardens provided much of the food for both local residents and visitors. Operating plantations moreover extended to the
town limits. Still, there were enough features of genuine town life--the presence of a number of merchants and
craftsmen, the crowded public times, etc.--to insure that
the economic function of Williamsburg's slaves was distinctive from that of the plantation Negroes.

Of all the impressions which one forms from
reading through the newspaper advertisements that are the
chief source of information about slave occupations in
Williamsburg the one which stands out most strongly is

that of a preponderance of "domestic Negroes," slaves
who were engaged in all the usual tasks of running a
household. Advertisements for the sales of lots of
Negroes were likely to specify that they were "valuable
Slaves, chiefly House Servants" or "valuable Slaves, being the servants usually employed in and about the house
and kitchen."[1] Where listings of such slaves stated the
skills and occupations of each, various domestic serv-
ants--cooks, waiters, slaves accustomed to general house
work, etc.--predominated. There is a measure of statis-
tical evidence for the large number of domestic slaves.
In a group of 104 Negroes chosen at random from among
those sold in Williamsburg at various times, advertisements for the sale of 60 give information about their previous work. Out of the 60 a total of 47 had been domestic servants of one type or another as against 13 craftsmen. This is not a large sampling, but it is at least a
clue to the proportion of household slaves in the general
slave population.

Many of the slaves, both male and female, used
for domestic work were simply general house workers--"House

---

1. _Virginia Gazette_ (Dixon and Hunter), December 23,
1775; (Purdie and Dixon), April 5, 1770.

Wench" was the most frequent term used to describe the women so employed. For example, among the 47 household slaves tabulated above 23 were advertised as experienced in general house work. This did not necessarily mean that they were the least skilled domestics. A good "house wench" could often perform any number of tasks, such as the one who understood "cooking, making paste, pickling, washing, ironing, cleaning house, and spinning."[2] Another was "well qualified for all Sorts of House-work, as Washing, Ironing, Sewing, Brewing, Baking &c."[3] A Negro boy of 18 whom Robert Nicolson advertised for sale in 1778 had been "used to the house ever since a child" and was especially good at cleaning or waiting table.[4]

There were, however, other house slaves trained for one or two specific duties. Logically only a relatively well-to-do owner would have the necessary hands to divide household labors too minutely. Where any degree of specialization occurred, it was usually the cook whose

2. Virginia Gazette (Rind), September 26, 1771.

3. Virginia Gazette, June 6, 1745.

4. Ibid.,(Purdie), March 20, 1778.

work was first separated from general household duties.

Probably personal menservants were next in frequency.

After that the division of labor might be made in a num-

ber of ways with slaves assigned especially to the laundry,

the garden, or the stables. It is surprising that in the

entire group of advertisements relating to Williamsburg

slaves no reference occurs to Negro women trained as per-

sonal maids for the ladies of the household. Below are

the specific occupations that are mentioned at one time

or another:

Nurse	Gardener
Washer and Ironer	Coachman
Cook	Hostler
Seamstress	Personal Manservant
Spinner	Waiter
Butcher	

Something has already been said of the abilities

of many slaves who were listed simply as general house

workers. The Negroes who performed more specialized jobs

were in many cases no less skilled. Phrases such as "ex-

ceeding good Washer and Ironer" or "exceeding fine cook"

occur frequently. To some degree these claims may be of

a piece with the twentieth-century used car dealer's ex-

travagant advertisement of his wares; but some of the de-

scriptions are almost too detailed to be completely

discredited. There was, for example, one young mulatto
woman, an experienced spinner and knitter, whom her master
claimed could "cut out and make up linen as well as any
servant in Virginia."[5] Others were well trained in two
or more types of work--a mulatto of 17 who was both a
waiter and a hairdresser; a Negro man of 25 trained as a
hostler, gardener, and house servant; or another man who
has waited on gentlemen but was also a tailor.[6]

Occasionally personal and household slaves of
really unusual qualifications turned up for sale in
Williamsburg. Sukey Hamilton, who had been Governor
Fauquier's cook before his death, was offered at public
sale on December 15, 1768.[7] Probably no slave could have
offered a wider range of qualifications than one who was
offered for sale as:

---

5. Virginia Gazette (Purdie), October 25, 1776.

6. Ibid., (Purdie and Dixon), July 11, 1773; (Dixon
and Hunter), March 30, 1776; (Purdie), June 7, 1776.

7. Ibid., (Purdie and Dixon), November 24, 1768.
The Rev. James Horrocks had purchased her from the Fauquier
estate at a relatively high price, and presumably it was he
who then sold her again in 1768, for reasons not known.
York County Records, Wills and Inventories, Book 22,
pp. 91ff.

> A very valuable young Negro man, who under-
> stands cleaning of a house, and is well
> qualified to wait on a single Gentleman, or
> a family, a very good gardener, and a tol-
> erable good cook, butcher, and plaisterer,
> and in short very handy at anything. He is
> also sober, very honest, and can play on the
> violin.[8]

The most remarkable of all, however, was:

> A Valuable young handsome Negro Fellow, about
> 18 or 20 years of age, has every qualification
> of a genteel and sensible servant, and has
> been in many different parts of the world. He
> shaves, dresses hair, and plays on the French
> horn. He lately came from London, and has with
> him two suits of new clothes, and his French
> horn, which the purchaser may have with him.[9]

A governor's cook, a man with a half dozen tal-
ents, or a world-travelled slave are admittedly well beyond the ordinary. However, even the more conventional
descriptions imply a high level of skill and experience.
With due allowance for the fact that most of these words
of praise come from advertisements, the impression still
remains that the domestic slaves of Williamsburg represented as able and well-trained a group of Negroes as
lived anywhere in the colony.

---

8. Virginia Gazette (Rind), October 19, 1769.

9. Ibid., (Purdie and Dixon), July 23, 1767.

Statistics in the preceding chapter indicated that easily five-sixths of the families in Williamsburg owned at least a single slave. With slaveholding so common, few households can have been without some domestic help. Nor can the possession of a few slaves to perform the house work have been much of a mark of social distinction in eighteenth-century Williamsburg. There must have been many modest homes in which one or two Negroes labored at every task from cooking and cleaning to gardening.

Even in the case of more prosperous citizens of Williamsburg, the number of slaves needed to maintain their households does not seem to have been excessively large. This is borne out by the fact that these men usually owned no more than ten to twenty slaves. George Wythe and Benjamin Waller, for example, held 14 and 13 respectively in 1783.[10] Francis Fauquier had evidently met the social demands of the governorship with a staff of 17 slaves, and five of these were small children.[11]

---

10. Williamsburg City, Personal Property Taxes, 1783.

11. York County Records, Wills and Inventories, Book 22, p. 91.

The comparatively large number of inns and ordinaries required for the busy public seasons of Williamsburg added a significant number of slaves trained for house work to the town's Negro population. Many of the inns appear to have operated much as any large household with about the same number of slaves and something of the same distribution of work. Anthony Hay, one of the keepers of the Raleigh, owned 20 slaves at the time of his death in early 1771.[12] When his estate was sold in March of that year, nineteen of the slaves, including "a very good Cabinet Maker, a good Coachman and Carter, some fine Waiting Boys, good Cooks, Washers, &c.," were offered for sale.[13] There are some other examples of innkeepers with roughly the same number of slaves, Henry Wetherburn, for instance, with an inventory of 13 in 1760 and James Southall with about 20 in the years just after the Revolution.[14] Many keepers of smaller establishments operated with a more limited number of slaves. One early

---

12. York County Records, Wills and Inventories, Book 22, pp. 19-24.

13. Virginia Gazette (Purdie and Dixon), January 17, 1771.

14. York County Records, Wills and Inventories, Book 21, p. 43; Williamsburg City, Personal Property Taxes, 1783-84.

innkeeper, Thomas Pattison, left an estate in 1742 that
included six slaves, two of them small children.[15] John
Burdett, who left six slaves in 1746; Henry Bowcock, five
in 1779; and Richard Charlton, seven in 1780 were similar
cases.[16]

The level of service that the slaves of Williamsburg's innkeepers provided may not have been uniformly
good, but at least one traveller found it highly satisfactory:

> In our hotel we had a very good though dear
> entertainment, Negro cooks, women waiters,
> and chambermaids made their courtesies with
> a great deal of native grace and simple ele-
> gance and were dressed neatly and cleanly.
> They yet recall and speak with evident de-
> light of the politeness and gallantry of the
> French officers.[17]

A number of Negroes were also employed for various housekeeping tasks at the College, apparently from a

---

15. York County Records, Wills and Inventories,
Book 19, pp. 177-179.

16. Ibid., Wills and Inventories, Book 20, pp. 46-48;
Wills and Inventories, Book 22, pp. 447-448, 469-470.

17. "A Journey from Philadelphia to Charleston, 1783."
Virginia State Library, quoted in Raymond B. Pinchbeck,
"The Virginia Negro Artisan and Tradesman," Publications
of the University of Virginia, Phelps-Stokes Fellowship
Papers, No. VII (Richmond, Va., 1926), p. 39.

very early date. It was a Negro man who went with Commissary Blair to force the doors of the grammar school in the celebrated "barring out" incident of 1702 and Governor Nicholson gave the College a Negro man valued at £30 in 1704.[18] In addition to its slaves in Williamsburg the College also owned Negroes on its lands along the Nottoway River.[19] Students also occasionally brought personal servants with them to Williamsburg. In 1754 there were eight slave boys at William and Mary, brought to wait on their young masters.[20]

Generally the College Negroes at Williamsburg worked under the direction of the housekeeper. One housekeeper, whose supervision was not all that the president and masters wished, was ordered in 1763 not to trust the Negroes with keys or to go away from the college too often, "As we all know that Negroes will not perform their

---

18. "William and Mary College Historical Notes," Manuscript Report, Colonial Williamsburg, pp. 95, 96, 99, 145.

19. Ibid., p. 235.

20. William and Mary Quarterly, 1st ser., VI (January, 1898), 187-188.

Duties without the Mistress's constant Eye especially in so large a Family as the College."[21]

It is not clear how many Negroes were normally used at the college, but in 1768 it was necessary to hire two extra ones for cutting and carting wood.[22] Three years later the college officials planned to purchase a Negro woman from Lord Botetourt's estate for college use.[23] It may have been more or less a regular practice to use some hired Negroes, because in the fall of 1777, when the president and masters decided to sell the land on the Nottoway and the slaves held there, they planned to bring two men and a boy from there to replace hired Negroes at Williamsburg.[24]

More elaborate changes occurred in December, 1779, as a result of the discontinuance of the grammar

---

21. Journal of Meetings of President and Masters, College of William and Mary, pp. 109-111.

22. Ibid., p. 167.

23. "William and Mary College Historical Notes," p. 202.

24. Journal of Meetings of President and Masters, pp. 269-270.

school and the Commons. The kitchen Negroes were to be leased to a steward who would contract to provide meals for students, a sufficient number of slaves were to be retained for cleaning, and any surplus ones were to be hired out at public auction.[25] It turned out that the steward was allowed two men and a boy and that five slaves were retained for cleaning.[26] Then in 1782 some of these remaining eight or else some of the ones offered for lease were to be sold to meet the cost of repairing the buildings.[27]

Predominant as the slaves engaged in domestic work were in the Negro population of Williamsburg, they did not entirely overshadow a smaller group of skilled and semi-skilled slave craftsmen. Such slaves appeared fairly frequently for sale here. Occasionally lots of Negroes were simply advertised as having "among them some good Tradesmen."[28] But more often than not skilled

---

25. Virginia Gazette (Dixon and Nicolson), December 18, 1779.

26. Journal of Meetings of President and Masters, p. 280.

27. Ibid., pp. 295-296.

28. Virginia Gazette (Purdie and Dixon), April 11, 1771.

craftsmen would be sold individually or singled out for special mention in an advertisement of a larger group of Negroes--an indication of a ready market for them. The demand, in fact, was great enough for the leasing of Negro artisans to become a profitable operation.[29]

In many cases slaves may have received such training as they had in a craft by the most informal sort of apprenticeship, perhaps working alongside some Negro craftsman and eventually absorbing whatever skill the older slave possessed. But it was also customary to bind slaves for a term of apprenticeship under a free craftsman.[30] Matthew Tuell, a carpenter living near town on Capitol Landing Road, had apprenticed to him in 1772 two Negro boys belonging to William Digges, Jr., of Yorktown.[31] In another instance, an unidentified purchaser sought to buy two other Negro boys for the specific purpose of

---

29. Virginia Gazette, September 12, 1745; (Purdie), November 24, 1775; January 10, 1777; December 5, 1777; December 12, 1777; January 19, 1778; March 27, 1778; (Dixon and Nicolson), July 24, 1779.

30. Pinchbeck, "Negro Artisan," pp. 29-30.

31. Virginia Gazette (Purdie and Dixon), June 11, 1772.

apprenticing them in some trade.[32]

Carpentry was rather clearly the most frequently practiced trade among Williamsburg's Negro artisans, as was also the case among plantation craftsmen throughout Virginia.[33] Shoemakers and blacksmiths were the next most often represented. There were, besides these three, at least an occasional slave trained in several other trades. Recorded evidence exists that the following crafts at one time or another were followed by slaves in Williamsburg:

Barber	Cooper
Blacksmith	Crafter
Butcher	Harnessmaker
Cabinetmaker	Shoemaker
Carpenter and joiner	Tanner
Carter	Tailor

Much of the information about Negro craftsmen in Williamsburg accords with a general pattern throughout the Southern colonies. Nevertheless, there are strong suggestions that neither the actual number of Negro

---

32. _Virginia Gazette_ (Dixon and Hunter), September 7, 1776.

33. Pinchbeck, "Negro Artisan," p. 32, for Virginia. The evidence for carpentry as the leading trade among Williamsburg slaves rests on its more frequent mention in issues of the _Virginia Gazette_.

artisans in the Virginia capital nor the range of crafts in which they were experienced was as large as elsewhere.

It has become a widely accepted view that such slaves became so numerous in many trades that white craftsmen in the South all but disappeared through emigration or change of occupation. In Charleston, where slaves became proficient in every craft including even that of jeweler, the white artisan class was virtually eliminated by 1790.[34] The same thing has been described as happening in Virginia, and it may well have on most plantations.[35] However, no suggestion of competition between white and Negro craftsmen in Williamsburg has as yet been found. No reference exists to laws here, as there were in South Carolina, that limited the number of Negro apprentices.[36] So far as we know, in the years in which Williamsburg flourished as the capital its white craftsmen remained a vigorous, flourishing group. Even as late as the 1780's, about thirty-seven remained.[37]

---

34. Leila Sellers, Charleston Business on the Eve of the American Revolution (Chapel Hill, N.C., 1934), pp. 102-105.

35. Pinchbeck, "Negro Artisan," pp. 25-26.

36. Sellers, Charleston Business, pp. 102-105

37. First Census of the United States...Virginia.

There is, of course, the possibility that competition between slave and free craftsmen might have been
eliminated, if a situation prevailed in which the white
artisans owned and employed Negroes skilled in the same
trade. One or two fairly clear examples of an operation
of this sort in Williamsburg do exist. During the early
years of the Revolution a carpenter and joiner named
Francis Jaram employed a number of helpers, some of them
slaves. He advertised at least twice in 1777 for sizeable
numbers of house carpenters and Negro carpenters.[38] He
leased some of the Negroes; but others were his own property. Jaram's slaves included a Negro carpenter named
Harry, advertised as a runaway in the spring of 1777
about the time his master was trying to acquire the additional slaves.[39] An interesting detail about Harry was his
master's observation that "when he works at a Bench he
works on the wrong Side." There was also in Williamsburg
a tan works, operated by William Pearson and employing

---

38. Virginia Gazette (Dixon and Hunter), March 21,
1777; (Purdie), July 25, 1777.

39. Ibid., (Dixon and Hunter), April 25, 1777.

four slaves who were experienced tanners and curriers, two shoemakers, and a carpenter.[40]

Jaram's and Pearson's methods, however, may be isolated examples. The average craftsman, it is true, seemed likely to own a few more slaves than the general run of Williamsburg slaveholders. A few examples include Alexander Purdie, the printer, who owned 13 at the time of his death; James Wray, a carpenter, with 20; Humphrey Harwood, a mason, with 10; and Peter Hay, an apothecary, with 11.[41] It turns out, however, in a number of instances that relatively few of their Negroes were adult males. And of those who were adult males, few have a high enough valuation in the inventory of the estate to make it appear that they were trained in their master's craft. Table No. 6 provides some illustrations of this point. The large proportion of female slaves and children, the small number of males, and the even smaller number of really valuable males suggest that the slaves belonging to craftsmen, much like those of other Williamsburg

---

40. Virginia Gazette (Dixon and Hunter), March 7, 1777.

41. The inventory of Harwood's estate is in York County Records, Wills and Inventories, Book 23, pp. 219-220. For the others, see below, Table No. 6.

Table No. 6

Adult Male Slaves of High Valuation in the Estates of Williamsburg Craftsmen

Reference in York County Records	Craftsman--	Craft	Year	Total Slaves	Adult Males	Males, High Valuation
W & I, Bk. 22, 330-37	Alexander Craig	Sadler	1776	8	1	1
O & W, Bk. 15, 562	David Cunningham	Barber	1719	7	1	0
W & I, Bk. 18, 587-88	Robert Davidson	Physician	1739	3	1	0
W & I, Bk. 23, 1-2	Cornelius Deforest	Baker	1782	6	4	1
W & I, Bk. 21, 444-48	Peter Hay	Apothecary	1769	11	1	1
W & I, Bk. 20, 364-66	Kenneth Mackenzie	Apothecary	1755	5	0	0
W & I, Bk. 22, 296-97	Matthew Moody	Cabinetmaker	1775	4	1	1
W & I, Bk. 22, 437-42	Alexander Purdie	Printer	1779	13	3(?)	2
W & I, Bk. 20, 204-08	James Wray	Carpenter	1750	20	7(?)	3
				72	18	9

residents, were largely domestics. There is some additional support for this supposition in the compilation of _Virginia Gazette_ advertisements already discussed above. There, it will be remembered, the Negroes identified as craftsmen numbered only about a fourth as many as those known to be household servants, 13 out of a total of 104 to be exact.

Moreover, the dozen or so crafts in which Williamsburg's Negroes are definitely known to have been employed are small in comparison with those in which slaves elsewhere in Virginia and in the other colonies engaged. Easily fifty different skilled occupations of Virginia plantation Negroes can be counted from the _Virginia Gazette_.[42]

There are few indications of the level of ability of the slave artisans who worked in Williamsburg. Occasionally there is a reference to an exceptionally skilled Negro. William Trebell, who lived near Williamsburg, owned a 26-year old slave, Bob, who was described

---

42. Lester J. Cappon and Stella F. Duff, (eds.), _Virginia Gazette Index, 1736-1780_ (Williamsburg, Va., 1950), II, 1076-1080.

in the following terms: "He is an extraordinary sower, a tolerable good carpenter and currier, pretends to make shoes, and is a very good tailor."[43] Lewis, a youth of only 18 or 19, belonging to Richard Wynne from near Yorktown, was an accomplished shoemaker.[44] Both these slaves were runaways, and both were successful in passing themselves off as free men. Lewis had called himself Lewis Roberts and remained as close to home as Williamsburg.

There is a suggestion in the use of the term "Negro carpenter" that Negro artisans were not always so skilled. As employed, it seems to denote not just a slave who happened to be a carpenter but a worker whose abilities were less than those of a white artisan. Francis Jaram, for instance, had sought in the same advertisement to hire "good house carpenters" and "Negro carpenters."[45] One suspects there is a precise distinction here that would have been quite clear to those who

---

43. Virginia Gazette (Purdie and Dixon), April 16, 1767.

44. Ibid., (Dixon and Hunter), July 10, 1778.

45. Ibid., (Dixon and Hunter), March 21, 1777.

read his announcement. Other advertisements employed the same term or spoke of a slave as being a "tolerable good carpenter."[46] It may well have been that most of the slave carpenters here--and they were the most numerous of the Negro artisans--were more nearly semi-skilled than skilled laborers.

Slave labor was also employed in two relatively large-scale undertakings in Williamsburg which went beyond the usual craft operation. The first of these was the vineyard established by public authority under the direction of a French winemaker, Andrew Estave.[47] It included a tract of about 200 acres located a mile and half outside town. Negro slaves were purchased with public funds to cultivate the vines, and through the years of actual operation Estave seemed to have an unusual amount of difficulty with runaways.[48] Then in March, 1777, both the land and the slaves were put up for sale.

---

46. Virginia Gazette (Purdie and Dixon), November 4, 1773; (Purdie), September 6, 1776.

47. Ibid., (Purdie), February 28, 1777.

48. Ibid., (Purdie and Dixon), October 22, 1772; November 18, 1773; March 24, 1774; (Pinkney), October 13, 1774; (Dixon and Hunter), March 23, 1776.

The disruption of trade during the American Revolution resulted in the establishment of the Manufacturing Society of Williamsburg, in effect a small factory utilizing slave labor. In the fall of 1776 it prepared to undertake the weaving of cloth, advertising for a superintendent and some spinners and weavers.[49] The following February the society sought a number of slaves and also indicated it would accept Negro girls as apprentices.[50] The Negroes that the society wanted to purchase included five or six Negro boys from 15 to 20 years of age, a similar number of girls from 12 to 15, and one or two weavers. The slaves employed at the Manufactory, as it came to be called, were soon producing some quantity of fabric, as four hundred yards of "hempen linen" plus a piece of imitation corduroy were offered for sale in the summer of 1777.[51]

It fell to the lot of the Negro in Williamsburg, as everywhere else, to perform the most difficult or the

---

49. Virginia Gazette (Purdie), September 6, 1776.

50. Ibid., (Dixon and Hunter), February 7, 1777.

51. Ibid., (Purdie), July 25, 1777.

most menial tasks. In town, where the slave was spared
the more demanding labor in the fields, his normal duties
as a household servant or as an artisan may seem a light
burden. Still, it would be a mistake to underestimate
the endless amount of drudgery required to make an eighteenth-century household function. The slaves here in
Williamsburg, however, proved themselves capable of developing a high level of ability. This applied especially to the best of the household slaves, although there
were examples of skilled Negro craftsmen.

In the light of the wide employment of Negro
artisans throughout the Southern colonies the degree to
which household servants seem to outnumber craftsmen in
Williamsburg is surprising. One result of this was to
reduce the importance of the slaves as a factor in the
economic life of Williamsburg. Their function was primarily one of personal service. For this very reason,
however, no representation of the everyday life and work
of Williamsburg would be completely accurate, if it did
not depict the slaves engaged in their daily round of
household duties.

Chapter VI

THE AUCTION BLOCK: WILLIAMSBURG AS A SLAVE MARKET

No single feature of slavery arouses more unpleasant reactions than the buying and selling of men
and women, as if they were so many livestock. The auction block was, however, an inescapable consequence of
having slavery at all; and Williamsburg could hardly be
free of this aspect of slave life. The capital had its
favorite spots for public sales, and few weeks went by
in which there was not some trading in Negroes.

A large proportion of the advertised sales of
slaves in Williamsburg were simply casual offers to dispose of a single Negro, or, at the most, two or three.
Forerunners of the present-day classified advertisements,
the listings of these slaves in the Virginia Gazette soon
fell into a stereotyped format.[1] Usually such notices

---

1. See, for example, Virginia Gazette (Purdie and
Dixon), September 29, 1774; (Dixon and Hunter), Janu-
ary 28, 1775; (Purdie), March 8, 1776; (Dixon and Hunter),
August 24, 1776.

did not identify the seller, and they almost never indicated either the price or reason for selling.[2] There
would simply be a brief description of the Negro involved,
and the interested purchaser was expected to "apply to the
Printer" for details. The actual sale in these cases was
presumably negotiated privately between owner and buyer
without resort to public auction. It seems that such
sales would almost certainly have involved only individual slave owners who for any number of reasons--a pressing debt, for example--may have found it necessary to dispose of a Negro or two. Such transactions can hardly
have had any great commercial significance.

A far greater number of Negroes changed hands,
however, at public sales which occurred with great frequency in Williamsburg. While there were a number of occasions for these auctions, they almost all shared the fact
that they were actions at law. The most common purpose, for
instance, was to settle the estate of a deceased resident.
In just over half the cases in which the occasion for a

---

2. One of the few advertisements to include an asking price was inserted by Robert Nicolson in the Virginia
Gazette (Purdie), for March 20, 1778. Nicolson asked £150
sterling for a Negro boy of 18 who was an experienced house
servant.

sale is specified, the slaves up for auction were part of an estate. Sometimes they were offered along with the rest of the personal property of the deceased and at other times were held for separate sale.

Most of the remaining public sales of Negroes were held to settle judgments of the courts, most often of the county court for James City. Occasionally there was also a sale held on order of the York County Court.[3] In a few cases the General Court as well ordered the Negroes sold:

> By virtue of a decree of the Hon. the General
> Court, obtained by Mess. Capel and Osgood
> Hanbury, of London, against Col. Philip Rootes,
> will be sold, for ready money, before Mr. Hay's
> door, in Williamsburg, the 16th of this instant
> (June) eight valuable NEGROES.[4]

Like Col. Rootes' slaves many of the Negroes involved in these court sales had been seized to pay their masters' debts.

New occasions for the selling of slaves by legal directive arose during the Revolution, when it is possible to find slaves, the late property of a fleeing

---

3. Virginia Gazette (Purdie and Dixon), September 22, 1768.

4. Ibid., (Purdie and Dixon), June 8, 1769.

Loyalist, being advertised for auction on the order of the Committee of Safety.[5] Nor did the Patriots overlook Lord Dunmore whose Negroes and personal estate were sold at the Palace.[6]

Except for a few instances in which persons leaving Virginia to return to England or to move elsewhere advertised their slaves, one or the other of the above legal actions were the only reasons ever advanced for various public auctions in Williamsburg.[7] There were, of course, sales from time to time for which no explanation was offered. But the typical public auction of slaves in Williamsburg was likely to be an executor's or a sheriff's sale.

Though the Market Square might have seemed a logical choice, there was no established slave market in colonial Williamsburg. By the nineteenth century an auction

---

5. Virginia Gazette (Purdie), June 7, 1776.

6. Ibid., (Dixon and Hunter), June 22, 1776.

7. In 40 Virginia Gazette advertisements, in which the occasion for a sale of slaves is explained, 23 such sales were settlements of estates, 13 were settlements of judgments of the courts, and 4 were sales of the property of persons leaving the colony.

block stood on the Court House Green; and the auctioneer's
cry, "Here they go," could regularly be heard there.[8]   But
in the eighteenth century far and away the favored location was the front of the Raleigh Tavern, one more indication of the Raleigh's pre-eminence as a busy center of Williamsburg life.   Once in a while another tavern served--
Gabriel Maupin's, Trebell's or some other.[9]   A few sales
also took place at the James City County Court House.[10]
Sometimes the public sale of an estate was held at the
home of the deceased, since the house itself and the furnishings might also be up for sale. Executors just as
frequently, however, had the slaves and other portions
of the estate auctioned at the Raleigh. All in all, the
Raleigh had an unrivalled position as the customary slave

8. Eliza Baker, "Memoirs of Williamsburg, Virginia,"
Typescript of conversation between Eliza Baker, an ex-
slave, and W. A. R. Goodwin, May 4, 1933, in Colonial
Williamsburg Archives, p. 5.

9. Virginia Gazette, October 17, 1752; (Purdie and
Dixon), December 4, 1766; (Dixon and Hunter), February 25,
1775.

10. Ibid., (Rind), June 29, 1769; (Pinkney), December 29, 1774; (Purdie), January 24, 1777.

market for Williamsburg all through the eighteenth century.[11]

There would seem to have been financial advantages in fixing the date of a sale of slaves during meetings of the General Court whenever possible. Nevertheless, there is no clear evidence that these crowded occasions were particularly favored. In two recorded instances sales were, however, advertised to take place during the Meeting of the Merchants,[12] but in one case several slaves experienced in handling river craft were offered and in the other, a serving boy being brought down from Tappahannock by a merchant. So these were both sales of special interest to the merchants. There were also some auctions during oyer and terminer court sessions.[13] But for the most part, if Negroes were to be sold on a court day, it was more likely to be a meeting

---

11. Of 62 sales in which the location is specified 37 took place at the Raleigh, 14 at private homes, 5 at other taverns, and 4 at the James City County Court House.

12. Virginia Gazette (Purdie and Dixon), October 28, 1773; October 20, 1774.

13. Ibid., May 12, 1738; October 15, 1752.

of one of the local courts, probably the James City county
court.[14]

One of the most difficult things of all to determine is the price which Negroes generally brought in
Williamsburg, since it was not customary to give a price
wanted in advertising Negroes for sale in the Gazette and
since nothing survives in the way of records of the level
of prices at auctions. William Campbell, a militia offi-
cer from western Virginia, wrote in complaint of the
prices around Williamsburg in early 1776:

> Negroes are exceeding dear in this part of the
> Country; 100 pounds and from that to 130 or 140
> is given for Negroe wenches; indeed I think
> they can be bought much cheaper in any of the
> back Counties than here--[15]

Prices had, by the time Campbell wrote, already begun the
inflationary spiral of the Revolutionary years. They continued to climb in terms of current money to the point
that assessors of estates in Williamsburg by 1779 valued

---

14. Virginia Gazette (Purdie and Dixon), June 18,
1767; July 25, 1771; (Rind), June 29, 1769; (Purdie),
January 24, 1777.

15. January 15, 1776, Campbell-Preston Papers,
Manuscripts Division, Library of Congress (Colonial
Williamsburg microfilm), I, 60.

the average adult male slave as a figure of around
£1000.[16] In the more stable situation which prevailed
before the Revolution a good male slave in Virginia is
supposed to have brought about £28-£35 sterling in the
first half of the eighteenth century and about £40
sterling after mid-century.[17] The assessments for inventories of estates in Williamsburg indicate a slightly
steadier rise:[18]

Year	Estimated Average Value of Adult Male Slaves
1740's	£40
1750's	£50-£60
1770-1771	£60-£75
1775	£100

These valuations from inventories of estates
are, of course, estimates; and it would be helpful to
know whether the public sales of the Negroes so inven-
toried brought in less or more money. The one estate
for which there seems to be such a record is that of

---

16. York County Records, Wills and Inventories,
Book 22, pp. 437-442.

17. Donnan, (ed.), Documents, IV, 6-7.

18. These estimates are based on a comparison of
the inventories of Williamsburg estates available in the
York County Records.

Governor Fauquier, and in every case his slaves sold for less than the amount for which they were listed in the inventory:[19]

Slaves	Value in Inventory	Purchase Price	Purchaser
John[20]	£ 40	£ 30	Thomas Everard
Bristol	55	41	Thomas Everard
Sukey and 2 children	140	105	Jas. Horrocks
Lancaster	70	52.10	Chris. Ayscough
Tidus	55	41.5	R. C. Nicholas
Tom		45	John Dixon
Mary and 1 child	70	52.10	John Dixon
John, Sall and 2 children	130	104	Geo. Gilmer
Moll	40	30	Richard Johnson
Nanny and 1 child (child died and discount allowed in purchase)	65	41.5	James Geddy

The clearest impression that emerges from what is known about the buying and selling of slaves in Williamsburg is that the town was never in the colonial period a slave market of any size or commercial importance.

---

19. York County Records, Wills and Inventories, Book 22, p. 91ff. Fauquier had moreover specified that the slaves should, where possible, go at less than the market value to the master of their own choice.

20. There is both a Young John and an Old John in the inventory with valuations of £60 and £40 respectively. The relative sale prices suggest that Everard purchased Old John.

The sales that went on here, frequent as they were,
turned out to be almost exclusively legal rather than
economic in motive. To be sure, the sellers intended to
realize as much of a financial return as possible; but
the sale arose in the first place out of some legal ne-
cessity--an estate to be settled, a debt to be discharged
by court order, or something similar.

Commercial traffic in slaves in the eighteenth
century usually suggested first of all the slave ship
landing its cargo of raw Negroes direct from some spot
on the African coast. Trade in imported slaves also included Negroes from the West Indies who came in smaller
numbers, though in more frequent shipments.[21] This entire foreign commerce in slaves was one in which Williamsburg did not seem to figure. The Naval Office for
the Upper James was located here so that cargoes of Negroes which were to be sold in that customs district
should have been registered in Williamsburg.[22] But there

---

21. Donnan, (ed.), *Documents*, IV, 183-234.

22. Two ships, the *Rae Galley* and the *Lilly*, were
seized and condemned by an Admiralty Court in Williamsburg
on October 5, 1769, for failure to register their cargoes
of slaves with the Collector. They were sold, however, at
Martin's Brandon. *Virginia Gazette* (Rind), October 5, 1769.

is no existing record of recently imported Negroes be-

ing sold here as they were at Yorktown and at nearby

points on the James.[23] In fact, many of the advertise-

ments of Negroes offered for sale in Williamsburg make

a particular point of emphasizing that they were "Virginia

born," the expectation being that Negroes born in the col-

onies were better trained and more valuable.[24]

There were still other characteristics which

made the market in slaves in the capital almost certainly

a local one. County court days were more popular as the

date of a sale than the times when the General Court was

sitting. The slaves auctioned here seem to have nearly

all been locally owned. In only a few cases did they

come from any distance. There are the two instances in

which slaves were brought in to be sold at the Meeting of

the Merchants.[25] Then in 1773 the sheriff of Middlesex

---

23. See, for example, Virginia Gazette, August 9,
1736; June 8, 1739; and October 27, 1752, for Yorktown.
For Bermuda Hundred on the James, see, ibid., (Purdie and
Dixon), September 5, 1766; August 11, 1768; May 18, 1769.

24. Ibid., October 17, 1752; (Purdie and Dixon),
December 18, 1766; March 31, 1768.

25. See above, p. 84.

County delivered "A Large Parcel of Young Virginia born
Slaves" to Williamsburg for sale at the Raleigh on
April 30.[26] Perhaps Williamsburg prices were already
so notoriously high that Middlesex decided to capitalize
on the situation. But with the evidence now available,
this stands as an isolated case.

A final argument against any large-scale com-
merical dealing in slaves in Williamsburg is the small
number of Negroes involved in the average public sale.
Quite commonly there would be only a single Negro to be
auctioned; and in many other cases only two or three
were sold at one time. Out of a total of 76 advertised
sales, in which the number of slaves to be offered is
definitely stated, 8 listed between 10 and 20 slaves; 6
listed 20 to 30; and only 2 mentioned a larger number.
The two largest were each auctions of about 50 slaves,
which is a sizeable enough number to raise the possibility that a merchant might have been involved. One
of these sales, however, was a York County Sheriff's sale
of "ABOUT fifty choice SLAVES, men, women, boys, and

---

26. Virginia Gazette (Purdie and Dixon), April 22,
1773.

girls; belonging to <u>Armistead Lightfoot</u>, and taken in
execution to satisfy several judgments of <u>York</u> court."[27]
There simply was not in Williamsburg enough trading in
slaves on a scale large enough to interest the merchants
of the colony.[28]

There is a certain contradiction in emphasizing how frequent and commonplace the public auction of
slaves must have been in Williamsburg and then saying
that so brisk a market in Negroes was really lacking in
economic significance. Yet no other summarization of
what we know about the buying and selling of slaves in
Williamsburg fits the available evidence. The citizen
of Williamsburg who found himself in need of an additional servant or two did not turn to the captain who
advertised that he was "lately arrived from the Gold
Coast, with a Cargo of choice Slaves." Instead he probably would have joined his neighbors and acquaintances

---

27. <u>Virginia Gazette</u> (Purdie and Dixon), September 22, 1768.

28. L. B. Steuart to Benjamin Massiah, July 5,
1751, Steuart Papers, Historical Society of Pennsylvania
(Colonial Williamsburg microfilm). This letter comments
very interestingly on the preference of merchants and
planters for large consignments of slaves.

who had gathered for a sale held by the sheriff,

Frederick Bryan, "at 12 o'clock before the Raleigh

Tavern for ready money of Several likely Slaves, to

satisfy some executions."[29]

---

29. Virginia Gazette (Purdie and Dixon), March 16, 1767.

Chapter VII

A PERSONAL DESCRIPTION OF WILLIAMSBURG'S NEGROES

Such details as the physical appearance, dress, or speech of the eighteenth-century slaves may seem almost more subjects of antiquarian curiosity than of real historical consequence. They cannot have mattered greatly to slaveowners who sometimes were hard pressed for an accurate description of one of their Negroes. However, there are a few general points of information that could contribute to the accuracy of any attempt to interpret the life of colonial Williamsburg's slave population.

Physically, the Negroes of the eighteenth century, like the whites of the same period, appear to have been on the average shorter in height than their modern counterparts. Both male and female slaves are sometimes described vaguely as being tall or tall and slim, but the instances are rare in which a Williamsburg slave is specifically estimated to be as tall as six feet.[1] In

---

1. Virginia Gazette (Purdie), July 25, 1777.

the largest number of instances adult males were stated
to be about 5 feet 5 inches or 5 feet 6 inches in height.[2]
Examples of slaves either slightly above or below this
figure occur about equally so that 5 feet 6 inches is a
reasonably accurate estimate of the average height of a
full-grown male Negro in eighteenth-century Williamsburg.

There is little reason to question the fact that
the clothing worn by Negroes was ordinarily of the simplest, coarsest variety.[3] One or two other assumptions
that are frequently made--that slaves were inadequately
clothed for winter weather and that the whites were care-
less about the outright nakedness of some slaves--have a
degree of accuracy but are not uniformly true. At any
one time most slaves probably had little more clothing
than what they were actually wearing. At least the occasional advertisements which describe a Negro with extra
clothing seem to make a special point of this fact.[4]

2. See, for example, Virginia Gazette (Purdie and
Dixon), March 24, 1774; (Purdie), March 8, 1776; (Dixon
and Hunter), March 23, 1776; July 20, 1776.

3. The Negro in Virginia. Compiled by the Writers'
Program of the Work Projects Administration (New York,
1940), pp. 71-73.

4. Virginia Gazette (Dixon and Nicolson), July 24,
1779.

In general one feels that the slaves in Williamsburg were reasonably well-clothed. The nature of the work most of them performed required fairly clean and adequate clothing. There are particularly favorable comments on the fact that waiters and cooks in the inns "were dressed neatly and cleanly."[5] To require that "the Negroes at the Better public houses must not wait on you unless in Clean shirts and drawers & feet washed--" more than met, however, the minimum demands of the eighteenth century in matters of cleanliness and dress.[6] Not every traveller was so well satisfied, as Ebenezer Hazard's complaint about the nakedness of Negro children on the streets of Williamsburg suggests:

> The Virginians, even in the City do not pay
> proper Attention to Decency in the Appear-
> ance of their Negroes; I have seen Boys of
> 10 & 12 Years of Age going through the Streets
> quite naked, & others with only Part of a

---

5. "A Journey from Philadelphia to Charleston, 1783."
Virginia State Library, quoted in Raymond B. Pinchbeck,
"The Virginia Negro Artisan and Tradesman," Publications
of the University of Virginia, Phelps-Stokes Fellowship
Papers, No. VII (Richmond, Va., 1926), p. 39.

6. William Hugh Grove Diary, University of Virginia
(Colonial Williamsburg photostat.)

Shirt hanging Part of the Way down their Backs.
This is so common a sight that even the Ladies
do not appear to be shocked at it.[7]

Whenever accounts occur describing the dress of
slaves from Williamsburg, the men are typically attired
in pants and a shirt plus a coat of some type. There is
a wide variety of fabrics, though all of coarser types,
and a whole rainbow of colors. The pants are once or
twice described as short breeches.[8] One of the most interesting variations was a pair worn by a man who had
run away so frequently that he was kept in leg irons.
His breeches were laced on the side so that they could
be worn over the irons.[9] The women seem usually to have
worn a petticoat and a dress of simple, colored material,
or else they are described as having on a petticoat and
a waistcoat.

Much of the lighter clothing for slaves was
made from cotton cloth woven in the colony, which was

---

7. Fred Shelley, (ed.), "The Journal of Ebenezer
Hazard in Virginia, 1777," Virginia Magazine of History
and Biography, LXII (October, 1954), 410.

8. Virginia Gazette (Dixon and Hunter), March 7,
September 5, 1777.

9. Ibid., May 9, 1745.

often called "Negro cotton" or "Virginia cloth."[10] A

certain amount of "country linen" was also produced here.[11]

English osnaburg, a heavy, coarse fabric, was also widely

used, as was another heavy material, Russian drab.[12]

In many cases the slaves in Williamsburg, as

they did everywhere else, wore old clothes, well-patched

and maybe passed down from the master's family.[13] But

there were new shirts and jackets interspersed among the

worn clothes, and a few slaves appear as very well-

dressed.[14] A fifteen-year old boy advertised as a runaway

in the winter of 1773 was wearing a new bearskin jacket,

blue breeches, country-knit stockings, and a light pair

of shoes with straps.[15] Alexander Purdie owned a runaway

---

10. Virginia Gazette (Purdie), September 6, 1776;
October 17, 1777; (Dixon and Hunter), March 21, 1777.

11. Ibid., (Dixon and Hunter), March 21, 1777.

12. Ibid., (Dixon and Hunter), July 20, 1776.

13. Ibid., (Purdie and Dixon), March 31, 1768;
(Dixon and Hunter), July 20, 1776; March 21, 1777;
September 5, 1777; (Purdie), October 17, 1777.

14. Ibid., (Purdie and Dixon), March 31, 1768;
(Dixon and Hunter), March 21, 1777.

15. Ibid., (Purdie and Dixon), January 7, 1773.

whom he described as "well-clad in new coat, waistcoat, and breeches, of red duffil, and has a new gray fearnaught great coat."[16]

One of the most misunderstood facts about the Negroes of the eighteenth century is the relative skill with which they spoke English. The logic of the recent importation of so many slaves from Africa plus the impressions that have stemmed from Negro dialects of later years have fostered the idea that very few slaves in the colonial era spoke more than very broken English. This viewpoint also had contemporary support from a few travellers.[17]

Nevertheless, there is a greater weight of evidence for the contrary view that with opportunity and a very little time the Negro learned to speak English clearly.[18] References to Negroes who spoke broken English or did not understand it at all nearly always prove to

---

16. *Virginia Gazette* (Purdie), March 8, 1776.

17. Cf. J. F. D. Smyth, "Travels in Virginia in 1773," *Virginia Historical Register*, VI (April, 1853), 82.

18. Allen W. Read, "The Speech of Negroes in Colonial America," *Journal of Negro History*, XXIV (July, 1939), 247-258.

involve very recent arrivals from Africa.[19] At that, the
average imported slave often learned to speak comprehensible English within a few years, like Lewis Burwell's
man, Jumper, who had been in the colony two years but
could talk "pretty good English."[20]

The level of speech of Negroes born and brought
up in the colonies was almost uniformly high.[21] Hugh
Jones commented as early as 1724 that "the Native Negroes"
were among "the only People [in both England and the col-
onies] that speak true English."[22] Since so high a proportion of the Williamsburg Negroes were Virginia-born,
they should have generally spoken fluent English. A representative example is that of a slave Peres, who had
lived for many years around Williamsburg before eventually becoming the property of George Washington. Peres,

---

19. Read, "Speech of Negroes," pp. 247-258.

20. Virginia Gazette, April 21, 1738.

21. Read, "Speech of Negroes," pp. 247-258.

22. Grace W. Landrum, "The First Colonial Grammar
in English," William and Mary Quarterly, 2nd ser., XIX
(July, 1939), 282. The work referred to and quoted from
is Jones' Accidence to the English Tongue (1724).

one of four slaves who engineered an escape from Washington in 1761, spoke good English, having "little of his Country Dialect left."[23] There were also a number of slaves here who were able to read and write without difficulty.[24] On the whole, this seems to be one more area in which the Negroes in Williamsburg were a superior group among the slaves of the colony.

---

23. Maryland Gazette, August 20, 1761.

24. Virginia Gazette, May 9, 1745; (Purdie and Dixon), April 16, 1767; February 21, 1771; (Purdie), December 12, 1777.

Chapter VIII

THE SOCIAL LIFE OF THE NEGRO IN WILLIAMSBURG

An oppressed community nearly always has a furtive quality about its life that conceals what its members really think and do and feel among themselves. This is simply a matter of self-preservation, of protecting whatever degree of independence its members still possess. Negro neighborhoods in the South have as often as not retained to the present day vestiges of such a barrier against white intrusions. As slaves the Negroes had even more need of this defense, and there are occasional evidences of the resourcefulness of the slave inhabitants of eighteenth-century Williamsburg in this regard.

No better example exists of the way in which the Negroes who lived here were both an integral part of the busy life of the capital and yet a society that could not be completely comprehended by their masters than the ability of the local Negro community to hide runaways.

It is perfectly clear that the Negroes who had lived here any length of time were well known to most of the white residents in the way of all small towns. Advertisers in the _Gazette_ often felt it unnecessary to tell more about a Williamsburg slave than the executors of Josiah Royle's estate did about a mulatto girl, Jenny, of whom they stated, "As she is well known in the Neighbourhood of this City, a more particular Description is unnecessary...."[1]

Yet Jenny and other Negroes just as well known were runaways who were thought to have remained in hiding in or around Williamsburg. In some cases a master only suspected that his slave had remained here secretly.[2] But there were other instances where slaves had been seen in Williamsburg since their "elopement" and still could not be recaptured.[3] Many of these fugitives had relatives or acquaintances in town whom the owners realized were

---

1. _Virginia Gazette_ (Dixon and Hunter), January 28, 1775. See also _ibid_., (Dixon and Nicolson), May 1, 1779.

2. _Ibid_., (Purdie), March 8, 1776; (Dixon and Hunter), March 23; September 5, 1776.

3. _Ibid_., (Rind), March 7, 1771; (Purdie), September 6, 1776.

probably hiding the fugitives.[4] William Carter, for instance, stated of his mulatto girl, Venus, who had run away in December of 1766, "I imagine she is either harboured by other slaves in kitchens and quarters in and about town, or else gone for <u>Nansemond</u> county, from whence she was purchased a few years ago."[5]

There was also difficulty with slaves who had once lived in Williamsburg and returned as runaways. Edward Cary, Jr. owned an 18-year old female slave raised in York County and leased to Philip Moody in Williamsburg in 1774. The next year Cary hired her out to John Thruston in King and Queen County; but Kate--this was the girl's name--had acquired attachments in Williamsburg that led her to flee Thruston's plantation. As Cary announced, "She has got a husband in <u>Williamsburg</u>, and probably may pass for a free person, as she is well acquainted in that city, and I have repeatedly heard of her being there."[6]

---

4. <u>Virginia Gazette</u> (Purdie and Dixon), September 15, 1768; January 10, 1771.

5. <u>Ibid</u>., (Purdie and Dixon), February 5, 1767.

6. <u>Ibid</u>., (Purdie), November 29, 1776.

It hardly seems possible that this slave girl could have
been a fugitive almost two years, have been recognized
frequently in Williamsburg during that time, and yet not
have been recaptured and returned to either Cary of
Thruston. Above all, she could hardly have succeeded,
unless the slave community had ways and means of shield-
ing its members that the slaveowner could not readily
penetrate.

Kate's experiences illustrate another feature
of the life of the Negro under slavery. She had run
away to Williamsburg in the first place because she had
a husband here, an important point for a number of reasons. The customs and practices of eighteenth-century
slavery did not usually permit the marriage of slaves,
even baptised ones, in any legal or religious sense.[7]
Yet for every slave who took advantage of, or was unable
to resist, the open invitation to promiscuity inherent
in such a situation, there were many others who tried
under the most difficult conditions to pursue a normal
family life. The slave owners gave a certain recognition

---

7. _The Negro in Virginia_. Compiled by the Writers'
Program of the Work Projects Administration (New York,
1940), pp. 79-85.

to these "marriages," although they often did not hesitate
to destroy a slave marriage by selling one mate.

There are even accounts of a sort of marriage
ceremony known as "jumping the broomstick," in which the
Negro couple stepped across a broomstick together as a
symbol of the fact that they considered each other husband and wife. One slave has left a personal recollec-
tion of her mother's broomstick marriage. As the mother
recounted it to her daughter, the young couple simply
decided on a Sunday that they would like to be married.
Thereupon they went up to the kitchen and asked to see
their master by sending word through the cook. After
determining they were old enough--both the boy and the
girl were 16 in this instance--the owner readily assented
and sent them off to one of the Negro women, Aunt Lucy,
who was probably either the midwife or the oldest woman;
and she performed the broomstick ceremony. ·Since it was
Sunday and all the Negroes were around their quarters,
the old woman called them together immediately. They
formed a circle around the couple, while Aunt Lucy re-
cited a few verses from the Bible and laid a broomstick
on the floor. The couple locked arms, jumped over the

stick, and were then husband and wife in the eyes of the
other slaves in the quarter.[8]

The slaveowners understandably preferred to
have their Negroes marry on the home plantation to lessen
the chance of runaways and to insure that children born
to the couple would belong to him. Permission to marry
on a neighboring plantation was sometimes granted, though
it usually restricted the couple to a single visit a week.[9]

It is only possible to speculate about the
problem slave marriages might create in a town such as
Williamsburg, where a large number of slaves belonging
to many different owners lived in close contact. The
number of unions of slaves belonging to different owners
undoubtedly increased, and the master's consent was probably much less vital than on an isolated plantation. He
was also likely to be able to do far less about destroy-
ing a marriage made against his will. These slave marriages may well have been the occasion of a lot of trouble
in Williamsburg. Certainly this is the source to which a

---

8. Negro in Virginia, pp. 81-82.

9. Ibid., p. 84.

large number of fugitive slaves can be traced. Edmund
Cary's Kate, whose flight from King and Queen to Williamsburg has already provided so much by way of illustration, had lived in Williamsburg only a year and yet
found a slave to whom she considered herself wed. Gaby,
a male slave belonging to James Burwell at King's Creek,
was listed twice in three years as a runaway.[10] Both
times he had fled into Williamsburg where his wife worked.
Slaves brought into Williamsburg from some distance and
thereby separated from a wife frequently ran off, too--in
this case not into hiding around town but back to their
original home.[11]

The frustrations that slaveowners experienced
in trying to recover slaves in hiding around town seems
all the more surprising in the view of the living arrangements for slaves. While our exact knowledge about where
slaves lived in Williamsburg is sketchy, we can be reasonably certain they lived on the master's property,

---

10. Virginia Gazette (Purdie and Dixon), September 15, 1768; (Rind), March 7, 1771.

11. Ibid., (Purdie and Dixon), January 8, 1767;
(Purdie), October 17, 1777.

perhaps close to the main house where surveillance should
have been relatively easy.

The conventional arrangement on the large plantations with one or two rows of crude slave cabins, possibly at some little distance from the plantation house,
was more extensive than even the larger town households
required. There were Williamsburg properties on which
undoubtedly an outbuilding or two was used specifically
for slave quarters. When a house that had belonged to
Peter Randolph was offered for sale, the description
pointed out that it included five major outbuildings--two
stables, a coach house, a kitchen, and a servant's house
of the same dimension as the kitchen.[12] One of the advertisements on runaways refers to "kitchens and quarters
in and about town," as if there might have been a fairly
large number of slave quarters scattered through Williamsburg.[13] In other cases the living space for slaves seems
not to have been a separate building but only the second-
floor rooms over the kitchens. Eliza Baker remembered

---

12. Virginia Gazette (Purdie and Dixon), October 8,
1767.

13. Ibid., (Purdie and Dixon), February 5, 1767.

slaves living over the kitchen at the Garrett House in the nineteenth century.[14] Household servants sometimes had no quarters of their own but simply spread pallets in the hall, on the staircase, or somewhere else in the house after the family had retired.[15]

Whatever the arrangement of living quarters for the slaves, they never were provided with much furniture. At best there can hardly have been more than a bed or a cot and maybe a few discarded pieces from the main house.[16] In the specific instance of Williamsburg not a single inventory has appeared that suggests anything definite about the furnishings of slave quarters. The inventory of the William Prentis estate did include a room-by-room listing of furnishings that also included outbuildings. It contains one or two entries of possible value. Described as being "In out House, Yard, &C" were a number

---

14. Eliza Baker, "Memoirs of Williamsburg, Virginia," Typescript of conversations between Eliza Baker, an ex-slave, and W. A. R. Goodwin, May 4, 1933, in Colonial Williamsburg Archives, p. 4.

15. Negro in Virginia, p. 42.

16. Ibid., pp. 67-69.

of tools, some scrap metal, and a few chairs and chests.
These last few pieces of furniture could have been used
by the slaves, although no beds at all were included.
Also, several items were "At old Nann[y's?]," one of
Prentis's slaves being called old Nanny. This included
only a frying pan, a pot, a grindstone, and a few tools,
however, and no furniture at all.[17]

The Negro slave had little time to spend as he
wished--usually Saturday nights and Sundays plus additional time at one or two major holidays like Christmas
and Whitsunday. Descriptions of plantation life substantially agree about the way in which the slaves spent their
spare time. On Saturday nights they usually gathered in
the slave quarters for dancing, which was as much their favorite recreation as it was that of most other Virginians.[18]
Philip Fithian has described how by five o'clock on Saturday at Nomini Hall "every Face (especially the Negroes)
looks festive & cheerful--"[19] Sundays the Negroes might

---

17. York County Records, Wills and Inventories,
Book 21, p. 253.

18. Negro in Virginia, pp. 87-95.

19. Hunter Dickinson Farish, (ed.), Journals and
Letters of Philip Vickers Fithian, 1773-1774: A Plantation
Tutor of the Old Dominion (Williamsburg, Va., 1943), pp.
180-181.

tend their garden plots or spend as much time as possible sleeping and resting.[20]

The slaves in Williamsburg probably enjoyed a social life that cannot have been much different, especially in amount of free time. Despite laws forbidding it, the Negroes here seemed able to procure and consume alcohol in some quantity. The Negro girl described as "fond of Liquor, and apt to sing indecent and Sailors Songs when so" is a good case in point.[21] So is the series of charges and countercharges involving the merchants Daniel Fisher, John Holt, and John Greenhow. Fisher was charged by the other two with selling liquor to Negroes without the written permission of their masters. When the case came into court, Fisher turned on his accusers and claimed that Holt had "without the least scruple whatever" served two Negroes whom Fisher himself had turned away. The aggrieved Fisher also claimed that John Greenhow was "infamously remarkable for trafficking with Negroes in

---

20. Fithian, Journal, p. 128.

21. Virginia Gazette (Purdie and Dixon), January 20, 1774.

wine, or any other commodity, Sunday not excepted."[22]
These accusations involve so much personal bickering and
name-calling that acceptance of them at face value is
impossible; but their general tenor suggests that a certain amount of dealing with slaves in liquor went on in
Williamsburg. Many of the masters may, for one thing,
have been lenient at times about issuing permission for
their slaves to have intoxicants. William Byrd recounted
the well-known instance in which Governor Spotswood could
not get his servants to remain sober for a large holiday
entertainment at the Palace until they were promised the
privilege of getting drunk the next day.[23]

Most of the aspects of life discussed above
would have been the private concern of a free person.
The slave, of course, had no such right. Where he lived,
whom he married, and sometimes even what he did for amuse-
ment were no more his to decide than the work he would do

---

22. "Narrative of George [Daniel] Fisher," William
and Mary Quarterly, 1st ser., XVII (January, 1909), 148-
149.

23. Louis B. Wright and Marion Tinling, (eds.),
The Secret Diary of William Byrd of Westover, 1709-1712
(Richmond, Va., 1941), p. 298.

or the master he would serve. Yet by a combination of
evasion and defiance the slaves were often able to
achieve some degree of independence in their social life.
Town life, if anything, seemed to increase this degree
of freedom and to create a slave community with its own
thoughts and pleasures and with the means of protecting
its fugitives.

Chapter IX

THE HUMANITARIAN IMPULSE: RELIGION AND EDUCATION

1. The Anglican Missionary Effort in Virginia

The first Negroes brought to Virginia came so largely by accident that there can hardly have been much thought one way or the other about Christianizing them. Religious motives played a part in colonization and in Indian relations, but only in retrospect did they become a justification for the importation of Negroes.[1] Nor were any sizeable number of blacks won to the Christian faith before the end of the colonial era.[2] Yet there were many ways in which religion was to influence the history of the Negro in these years.

---

1. Perry Miller, "The Religious Impulse in the Founding of Virginia: Religion and Society in the Early Literature," William and Mary Quarterly, 3rd ser., V (October, 1948), 492-522; VI (January, 1949), 24-41.

2. The best general discussion of this is Marcus W. Jernegan, "Slavery and Conversion in the American Colonies," American Historical Review, XXI (April, 1916), 504-527.

At first, when the few Negroes in Virginia were generally regarded as no different from other servants, a number of them were baptized, probably as a matter of course and without much thought on the part of the white settlers that it had any special significance. Anthony and Isabella, two of the Negroes in the original shipment, were married soon after their arrival; and their first child was taken to Jamestown in 1624 and baptized with the name of their master, William Tucker.[3] Another example was Rose, a Negro belonging to Robert Stafford, whose son William was baptized in 1655.[4] In the light of the Spanish Christian names borne by some of the earliest Negroes--the aforementioned Anthony and Isabella, two other Anthonys, a John Pedro, and others--some of them may have been baptized by the Spanish and then captured and brought to Jamestown.[5] Baptism probably carried some

---

3. The Negro in Virginia. Compiled by the Writers' Program of the Work Projects Administration (New York 1940), p. 10.

4. Joseph B. Earnest, The Religious Development of the Negro in Virginia (Charlottesville, Va., 1914), p. 18.

5. Helen T. Catterall, (ed.), Judicial Cases Concerning American Slavery and the Negro (Washington, 1924-1926), I, 54-57.

temporal advantages with it, as in the case of John Phillip, a Negro, who in 1624 was permitted to testify as a free man and a Christian because he had been baptized.[6] At the least it made it easier to incorporate the Negroes into the existing system of indentured servitude.[7]

As the status of the Negro began to harden into life servitude, however, the owners became increasingly afraid that baptism might result in freedom for their Negroes.[8] English precedent was not entirely clear, and some planters took the precaution of actively forbidding baptism of Negroes bound for life. In 1667 the Assembly broke the impasse by enacting legislation that baptism did not alter a person's bond or free condition. The same law also encouraged masters to permit capable slaves to be baptized.[9] Subsequently, whether one was black or

---

6. Catterall, Judicial Cases, I, 76.

7. Ibid., I, 54-55.

8. Jernegan, "Slavery and Conversion," pp. 504-507.

9. William Waller Hening, (ed.), The Statutes at Large Being a Collection of all the Laws of Virginia (Richmond, Va., etc., 1810-1823), II, 260.

white began to replace whether one was Christian or pagan as the true determining factor between free and slave status.[10]

The way now stood clear for the defense of slavery as a Christianizing and civilizing institution. The image of the rude, animal-like African being educated and humanized by the beneficent influences of bondage, not the least of which was religion, became a bulwark of the rationale for slavery.[11] This argument was not entirely conceived in hypocrisy. Many set out to give substance to the proposition that slavery might be a means of conversion of the Negro, for the English-speaking world was experiencing the dawning of a humanitarian

---

10. Hening, Statutes, II, 283, 490-492; III, 447-448.

11. Jernegan, "Slavery and Conversion," pp. 504-507. Here, however, the idea is advanced that the justification of slavery as a means of conversion preceded any fear that such conversion would free the Negro and that therefore missionary activity received a temporary setback. But it is doubtful that the argument that slavery offered an opportunity for propagating religious faith really became much of a factor until the status of a slave had been more sharply defined. By that time the possibility that Christianity might convey freedom had been resolved in favor of continued bondage.

impulse that was to make its full force felt only after 1800.[12] Its roots at this time were religious, and the primary concern of those who worried about the fate of the Negro was that his soul might be saved in the next world by conversion to Christianity in this. To a lesser extent they also wished to educate the slave, though primarily as a means of increasing his capacity for understanding religion.

The intent of the humanitarians in all their endeavors was not even remotely revolutionary. They were in all sincerity striving to improve the existing order. In their aspirations for the Negro they sought only to make slavery more humane, not to eradicate it as fundamentally and irrevocably inhuman. Religious training, they sometimes argued, would actually make the Negro more obedient and more satisified with his lot.[13]

Almost none of this interest in the slaves originated among colonial slave owners, and little of it

---

12. George Macaulay Trevelyan, English Social History (London, etc., 1947), p. 347.

13. Edgar L. Pennington, "Thomas Bray's Associates' Work Among Negroes," American Antiquarian Society Proceedings, new series, XLVIII (1938), 334-335.

represented governmental policy. The instructions of a new governor normally included a brief exhortation to encourage the conversion of Negroes, but official action just about stopped at that point.[14] The real source of endeavor was the Anglican Church. Until late in the eighteenth century the successes in converting and educating the Negro were the results of the Church's efforts and the failures were a reflection of the Church's limitations for so staggering a task.

The Church pursued its interest in the Negro. Through the eighteenth century most of the Bishops of London made it a point of special concern; and their commissaries in Virginia, especially James Blair and William Dawson, were in agreement. Sometimes this influence had the desired effect on the parish clergy, for more of them than one might have thought were seriously interested in attempting to reach the slaves within their parishes.[15] In the colonies as a whole the Society for

---

14. See, for example, Virginia Magazine of History and Biography, XXI (October, 1913), 354; XXVIII (January, 1920), 43.

15. There is a convenient summary of the Anglican effort in Virginia to convert the Negro slaves in Mary F. Goodwin, "Christianizing and Educating the Negro in

the Propagation of the Gospel, from its founding in 1701, expended a part of its missionary effort on the Negro, but very little of its work occurred in Virginia.[16] Dr. Bray's Associates, a smaller group especially interested in schools and libraries, was responsible for the operation of two Negro schools in Virginia.

One of the peak periods of Anglican missionary effort among the Negroes came in the decade of the 1720's, when Edmund Gibson, just consecrated as Bishop of London, threw his influence behind the movement. Gibson's correspondence to and from Virginia was filled with discussion of the slaves. One of the key questions in his questionnaire of 1724 to clergymen working in the colonial field was, "Are there any Infidels, bond or free, within your Parish; and what means are used for their conversion?"[17]

Colonial Virginia." Historical Magazine of the Protestant Episcopal Church, I (September, 1932), 143-152.

16. Edgar W. Knight, (ed.), A Documentary History of Education in the South Before 1860 (Chapel Hill, N.C., 1949-53), I, 63.

17. William Stevens Perry, (ed.), Historical Collections Relating to the American Colonial Church (Hartford, Conn., 1870), I, 261.

Three episcopal letters in 1727 on the conversion of Negroes intensified his campaign.[18] There were even proposals to make it economically attractive for the planters
to encourage religious instruction for their Negroes by
offering to exempt a slave baptized before the age of 14
from the tithe for four years.[19] These years represented
probably the most intensive campaign to win the conversion of the slaves at any time prior to the Great Awakening.

Of the clergy who answered Bishop Gibson's set
of questions only one or two flatly admitted they were
making no effort among the Negroes. The Rev. Owen Jones
of St. Mary's in Essex County replied cryptically that
in his parish, so far as the conversion of slaves was
concerned, "particular means [were] discouraged."[20] The
same thing was undoubtedly true of most of the clergy
who completely ignored the bishop's query.

---

18. Jernegan, "Slavery and Conversion," pp. 507-511;
Fulham Palace Manuscripts, Virginia, British Transcripts,
Library of Congress, II, 109.

19. Perry, Historical Collections, I, 344.

20. Ibid., I, 310.

The efforts of the more active ministers followed an almost uniform pattern. In the first place,
they regarded the newly imported African as beyond their
influence, as quite probably he was, unless he had mastered English very quickly. So, for the most part, they
confined their efforts to Negroes who had been born in
Virginia or had grown up there from early in life.[21]
The method of instruction was largely the time-worn one
of "preaching and catechising." Quite often there was
no special effort to adjust these instructions to the
needs and understanding of the Negroes. The slaves were
expected to get along on the regular sermons and whatever
teaching of the catechism the children of white parishioners received.[22] Usually about the time a slave could
recite the catechism and maybe the Apostle's Creed and
Lord's Prayer reasonably fluently, he would be baptized.[23]
Rarely and in extremely small numbers, slaves were admitted to the sacrament of the Holy Communion.[24]

---

21. Perry, Historical Collections, I, 264, 280, 283,
287, 293, 297, 312.

22. Ibid., I, 261, 271, 273, 281, 285, 308.

23. Ibid., I, 263, 274, 276, 280, 287, 291, 297, 301.

24. Ibid., I, 291.

Clergymen were careful to avoid the slightest hint of an attack on the institution of slavery. Many of the Virginia clerics were themselves slaveholders, and the Church also owned slaves which had been left it as endowments in the wills of deceased Virginians.[25] In their instructions the ministers urged the Negroes to cultivate obedience and patience as virtues becoming a Christian slave. Nothing was left undone to impress upon the slaves that Christianization was not to be confused with freedom in this world. In one instance Negroe candidates for baptism were required to take a special oath declaring that they did not seek baptism out of any design of freedom.[26]

The church still ran into uncompromising opposition from the slaveowning planters. Occasionally a minister was able to report:

> ...I have prevailed with some of my parish-
> ioners to suffer their slaves to be instructed
> in ye christian religion & baptized, for which
> they have since thank'd me, having found them

---

25. R. W. Marshall, "What Jonathan Boucher Preached," Virginia Magazine, XLVI (January, 1938), 4-6; Perry, Historical Collections, I, 360-361.

26. Pennington, "Thomas Bray's Associates," p. 333.

> both more trusty & more diligent in their
> service than they were before...[27]

But he was much more likely, when the subject of baptizing slaves was raised, to find "the owners Generaly not
approving thereof, being led away by the notion of their
being and becoming worse slaves when Christians."[28] Between the hostility and indifference perhaps a few families remained in a parish who were willing to permit instruction and baptism of slaves.

If the slaveowners needed a justification for
their position, they were able to find it in the rumors
of a slave insurrection on which Bishop Gibson's first
efforts foundered in 1730. The exact details of the incident are difficult to establish, as two letters, one
from Commissary Blair and one from the governor to the
Bishop of London are about the only sources.[29] Both
Blair and Gooch denied that there was any well-formed

---

27. Lawrence De Butts to Bishop of London, July 1,
1722, Fulham Palace Manuscripts, Virginia, I, 133.

28. Perry, Historical Collections, I, 315.

29. May 14 and May 28, 1731, Fulham Palace Manuscripts, Virginia, I, 110, 111.

plan of revolt, though Blair conceded that the Negroes had been circulating rumors that baptism would set them free and that they had grown "angry and saucy" when their day of liberation failed to arrive. There had been talk of insurrection and a certain amount of uneasiness on both sides. Then, according to Gooch, trouble appeared to subside for a few weeks only to reappear in Norfolk and Princess Anne Counties. There two hundred Negroes gathered to choose leaders for a rising, but an informant revealed their plot with the result that four of the ringleaders were hanged.

The missionaries were shortly back at work, however, with fresh hopes of converting the slaves. Their plan of attack was still essentially to preach and to catechise, though "in such a plain affecting way as may move their hearers."[30] These clergymen continued to meet strong opposition from their parishioners.[31] But occasionally they had phenomenal successes, as when the

---

30. Charles Bridges to Bishop of London, October 20, 1735, Fulham Palace Manuscripts, Virginia, II, 40.

31. Adam Dickie to Mr. Newman, June 27, 1732, Fulham Palace Manuscripts, Virginia, III, 39.

Rev. Anthony Gavin, rector of St. James, Goochland, baptized a total of 172 Negroes on a journey through the
far reaches of his parish.[32] Examples like this did not
occur frequently enough, though, for these men to begin
to keep pace with the expanding slave population.

It is easy to conclude that the ultimate failure of the Anglican effort to reach the slaves resulted
not only from the hostility of many planters but also
from lack of much real spirit among most of the clergy.
There is much support for this view in the indifference
of someone like the Rev. John Bell, who said of the Negroes in his parish, Christ Church, in Lancaster County,
"The Church is open to them, the word preached, and the
Sacraments administered with circumspection."[33] Well-
intentioned men were sometimes overcome by the immen-
sity of the task the bishop had asked of them and fell
into the weariness of Charles Bridges who once wrote to
his superior:

> The little good I find I am capable of doing
> without your particular countenance in first

---

32. Perry, Historical Collections, I, 360-361.

33. Ibid., I, 283.

subscribing and getting subscription to,
that your excellent design of instructing
the Negroes here according to the method
proposed, and pressing the Commissary to
follow you and solicit the Governor and
his interest, I say all that can be done
in this affair without your charitable
efforts, will, to my great concern, I fear
come to nothing. The Commissary and I grow
in years, and the world hangs heavy upon us.
I am rous'd sometimes and then call upon him,
and then he is asleep perhaps & answers nothing, & I am ready to sleep too. Would to God
your powerful voice would sound in our ears
to get up and be doing a little more good,
while there is time and opportunity,...[34]

There were, of course, ministers of greater
zeal and ability laboring in the same cause. Commissary
Blair, despite his age, was asleep less than Charles
Bridges seemed to think. Adam Dickie in Drysdale Parish,
King and Queen County, worked hard, holding separate Sunday morning classes for Negroes, because his white parishioners would not allow their children to recite the
catechism in the company of slaves. Moreover his very
realistic awareness of the difficulties involved did not
diminish his efforts.[35] Almost every parish recorded

---

34. Perry, Historical Collections, I, 360-361.

35. Adam Dickie to Mr. Newman, June 27, 1732,
Fulham Palace Manuscripts, Virginia, III, 39.

baptisms in small numbers; and in a few the numbers were surprisingly large, as in Accomac Parish when about two hundred Negroes received baptism within a brief period and in Northampton Parish, where 341 baptisms were once recorded in a single month.[36]

The fact of the matter is that the degree of spirit and sincerity behind the Anglican missionary drive among the slaves is not a matter for easy generalization. One could go on citing contrasting examples of indfference and zeal, but to no real purpose. The character of the Church's effort was, in fact, of minor consequence in its failure to win Negroes in large numbers. Had every clergyman in Virginia been tireless in this cause, they still would have ministered to a parish that might well have contained several thousand Negroes. They still would have faced the hostility of many slaveowners, who were little enough concerned about the place of religion in their own lives. They still would have been advocating that the slave live according to a moral code that

---

36. Perry, Historical Collections, I, 301; Fulham Palace Manuscripts, Virginia, III, 42.

was almost impossible to follow in an environment where,
for instance, there was no legal marriage.

In the long run, the humanitarians held an
illogical position in insisting upon maintaining slavery,
even defending it as a moral good, and yet claiming the
slave for a religious faith which elevated the worth of
a human as high as did Christianity. As long as they
held this view, they could go on hacking at the edges of
the problem, here and there converting a few favored
slaves owned by especially humane masters. But there was
an ultimate incompatibility between slavery and Christianity. The masters knew it with a sort of hard-headed
realism, and the slaves at least sensed it from the frequent spread of rumors about winning freedom through
baptism.

2. The Anglican Missionary Effort in Williamsburg

Williamsburg as the capital and residence of
the Bishop's Commissary could never expect to be long out
of touch with these currents of Anglican missionary effort.
In the years of Bishop Gibson's greatest activity James
Blair was serving both as Commissary and as rector of

Bruton Parish. Replying to the 1724 questionnaire Blair
had little to say about any success in converting the
slaves, but he assured the Bishop of his best efforts in
the following terms:

> I encourage the baptising & catechising of
> such of them as understand English, and ex-
> hort their Masters to bring them to Church
> and baptise the infant slaves when the
> Master or mistress become sureties.[37]

However, Blair and his successors at Bruton
seem to have had relatively more success over the years
in baptizing a portion of the slave population than did
many of the clergy in more rural parishes. Blair's correspondence with the Bishop always took an optimistic note,
as when he wrote in 1729:

> Your Lo'ps Letter concerning the Instruc-
> tion of the Negroes has had this good effect,
> that it has put several Masters and Mistresses
> upon the Instruction of them. And the Negroes
> themselves in our Neighbourhood are very de-
> sirous to become Christians; and in order to
> it come and give an Account of the Lords
> prayer, and the Creed and ten Commandments,
> and so are baptized and frequent the Church;
> and the Negro children are now commonly bap-
> tized. I doubt not some of the Negroes are
> sincere Converts; but the far greater part
> of them little mind the serious part, only

---

37. Perry, Historical Collections, I, 299.

> are in hopes that they shall meet with so
> much the more respect, and that some time
> or other Christianity will help them to
> their freedom. But I hope their very com-
> ing to church will in time infuse into them
> some better principles than they have had.[38]

And again the following year:

> There is a very great number of Negroes
> lately instructed in the Church-catechism; at
> least in the Lords prayer, the Apostles Creed
> and the ten Commandments, and baptized, and
> great numbers of them frequent the Church.
> Some allege it makes them prouder, and in-
> spires them with thoughts of freedom; but I
> take this to be rather a common prejudice
> than anything else.[39]

The parish records of Bruton show specific fig-

ures for Negro baptisms during most of the twenty-three

years between 1746 and 1768. In all, 980 slaves and a

few free Negroes received baptism during 19 of these 23

years.[40] There are two later years during the Revolution

when 32 and 69 baptisms respectively took place. Then

the number drops to almost nothing. By then the slaves

---

38. June 28, 1729, Fulham Palace Manuscripts,
Virginia, II, 109.

39. July 20, 1730, Fulham Palace Manuscripts,
Virginia, I, 131.

40. W. A. R. Goodwin, Historical Sketch of Bruton
Church (Petersburg, Va., 1903), p. 153.

may have been attending the independent Negro Church in
Williamsburg.[41]

The masters whose names are recorded as having
slaves baptized likewise constitute a long and rather
representative list. A few had sizeable numbers of their
slaves baptized at one time or another. Lewis Burwell
with 70 of the Kingsmill slaves baptized from 1747-68
easily led the list. Benjamin Waller had 39 of his slaves
baptized between 1746 and 1782; James Shield, 31 between
1747 and 1783; Col. Philip Johnson, 24 between 1747 and
1782; and there were others with almost as many. The
College was sponsor for 21 of its slaves. A large number of well-known men also were listed as the owners of
smaller numbers of baptized slaves, among them several
rectors of the parish; two governors, Gooch and Fauquier;
and the Treasurer, Robert Carter Nicholas, well-known for
his piety in many instances.[42]

Some of these men were, however, owners of a
large number of slaves; and it is doubtful just what

---

41. See below, section 5, of this chapter.

42. See Goodwin, Historical Sketch of Bruton Church,
pp. 154-157, for a complete listing of communicants having
Negroes baptized in the eighteenth century.

percentage of their slaves, or of the whole Negro community of Williamsburg, were afforded religious training and eventual baptism. Here, for example, is a sampling of masters for whom there is both a recorded inventory of their estate and a record of slaves baptized:

	No. of slaves at death	No. of slaves baptized
Alexander Purdie	13	3
Alexander Craig	8	6
Peyton Randolph	28	17
John Prentis	11	0
Matthew Moody	4	4
Thomas Cobbs	4	2
Joseph Valentine	12	2
Mark Cosby	5	2
James Wray	20	12
Frederick Bryan	34	16
Anthony Hay	20	5
Peter Hay	11	2
Nathaniel Crawley	32	12

There are a number of questions which these figures cannot answer, particularly that of how many slaves might have been bought after being baptized; but in only a single instance do the number of baptized slaves actually equal the number belonging to the owner at death. It would seem that slaveowners in Williamsburg, while not unsympathetic to the baptism of their slaves as some of the planters, still encouraged the step for only a portion of their Negroes. A thousand Negro baptisms in twenty

years is large enough, however, to prove that the clergy
of Bruton Parish did put forth some effort and that the
slaveowners of the parish were not always openly hostile
to religious instruction of slaves.

3. The Associates of Dr. Bray

Education in eighteenth-century Virginia was
at best a haphazard process, even for the children of
white parents who were financially able to provide for
the instruction of their children. It followed that formal education for Negroes was all but non-existent. It
was possible for the boys of free Negro parents to be
bound as apprentices on about the same basis as white
children. The surviving indentures for free Negroes are
largely identical with those of white apprentices in
their requirements of adequate training in the master's
craft and instructions in reading and writing.[43] Then,
too,the same group of humanitarians who labored for the

---

43. William and Mary Quarterly, 1st ser., VIII
(October, 1899), 82; Virginia Magazine, II (April, 1895),
429.

religious conversion of the Negro sought to give him at least enough education to comprehend simple religious training.

There is, for example, some evidence of interest in education for Negroes in Williamsburg as early as the 1740's. It is Commissary Dawson's name alone, however, which figures in the available evidence. On Dec. 22, 1743 he wrote to England asking for a copy of school rules "w^{ch}, with some little Alteration, will suit a Negro School in our Metropolis, when we shall have the Pleasure of seeing One established..."[44] Then only a few years later, in 1750, he wrote the Bishop of London about Negro schools, "There are three such schools in my parish, these I sometimes visit."[45] Whether these were no more than occasional catechism classes or more regular instruction is a complete mystery, though it hardly seems likely that they could have had a very long history without attracting wider notice. Perhaps one of them was taught by an Elizabeth

---

44. To William Newman, December 22, 1743, Dawson Papers, 1728-1775, Manuscripts Division, Library of Congress. (Colonial Williamsburg microfilm.)

45. W. A. R. Goodwin, The Record of Bruton Parish Church (Richmond, Va., 1941), p. 34.

Wyatt who billed Dawson's estate £1.6 in October, 1754,
for schooling his Negro girl, "Jinny," one year.[46]

In the 1760's the English philanthropic group
known as Dr. Bray's Associates decided Williamsburg was
worth a try as the location of one of its schools for Negro children. Out of this effort came a school about
which we know something more than these earlier ones.
Before his death in 1730 Thomas Bray, who had already
been a leader in establishment of the S.P.G., named a
group of trustees to work with him in "amongst ye Poorer
sort of people, as also among ye Blacks and Native Indians." After their founder's death the group decided to
perpetuate itself as the Associates of Dr. Bray. In time
it came to concentrate its efforts on supplying libraries
for Anglican parishes in America and in providing education for Negro children.[47]

The Associates at one time or another founded,
or attempted to found, Negro schools in a number of towns

---

46. Dawson Papers, Library of Congress.

47. Pennington, "Thomas Bray's Associates," pp. 315-326. See also H. P. Thompson, Thomas Bray (London, 1954), especially pp. 98-99.

and cities throughout the American colonies. The most
successful one operated in Philadelphia, for it was strong
enough to reopen after the Revolution and continue into
the nineteenth century.[48] None of the others came near
this record, but the school in Williamsburg operated as
long and as successfully as any of the remaining ones.

It was at a meeting of the Associates on January 17, 1760, in the usual London gathering place, "At
the Angle Ave Mary Lane," that the project for the school
in Williamsburg, together with ones in New York and Newport, was first proposed.[49] The suggestion as to locations came from Benjamin Franklin, who two weeks earlier
had taken his place as a newly elected member of the Associates.[50] Also on Franklin's recommendation, William
Hunter, postmaster in Williamsburg and printer of the

---

48. Pennington, "Thomas Bray's Associates," pp. 369-381.

49. Knight, (ed.), Documentary History of Education,
I, 141. For convenience of reference, this and many subsequent citations to the records of Dr. Bray's Associates
are from the printed text, edited by Edgar W. Knight. Colonial Williamsburg, however, also possesses microfilm copies
of the original records from the Archives of the Society
for the Propagation of the Gospel in Foreign Parts.

50. Knight, (ed.), Documentary History of Education,
I, 141.

Virginia Gazette, and Thomas Dawson, President of William and Mary and rector of Bruton Parish Church, were asked to become trustees for the Williamsburg school.

At the same meeting the Associates instructed one of their members, the Rev. James Waring, to prepare a shipment of books for each of the schools.[51] The books which were apparently sent in this first shipment included the following:

        50 Child's First Book
        40 English Instructor
        25 Catechism broke into Short Questions
        10 Easy Method of instructing Youth
        2 Preliminary Essays on the Exposition of the
            Catechism
        3 Indian instructed
        5 Bacons 4 Sermons addressed to the Planters
        2 Bacons 2 Sermons addressed to the Negroes
        10 Christians Guide
        12 Friendly Admonistions to the Drinkers of
            Spirit. Liq.
        3 Church Catechism with tracts of Scripture

        Allens Discourses
        Brays Lectures   bound
        Kettelwell's Practical Believer   together

        20 Sermons before the Trustees & Associates (by
            Bruce, Thoresby, King, Ridley)[52]

---

51. Knight, (ed.), Documentary History of Education, I, 142.

52. Minutes of Dr. Bray's Associates, Catalogue of Books for Home and Foreign Libraries, Manuscripts of Dr. Bray's Associates, S.P.G. Archives.

It fell to the local trustees for the proposed schools to do far more than lend their prestige to the undertaking or perhaps make an occasional inspection. In Williamsburg, for example, Hunter and Dawson had to organize the school, find a teacher and place for it to meet, and supervise its day-to-day operation. Since Thomas Dawson died just as the school in Williamsburg opened, Hunter undertook most of the responsibilities connected with the establishment of the school.

He engaged as a teacher Mrs. Anne Wager, who was to be the only instructor the school ever had.[53] The Associates had decided that £20 sterling would be an adequate salary, but Hunter thought she should have £30 out of which she would have to pay the rent on a suitable house for herself and the school.[54] Dawson had wished

---

53. We know little about Mrs. Wager. She was elderly, possibly the widow of Thomas Wager who died in Williamsburg in 1725. Her son-in-law was Matt Hatton, a carpenter who owned four lots on Capitol Landing Road and who received the wages still due her after her death. Mary A. Stephenson, "Notes on the Negro School in Williamsburg," Manuscript Report, Department of Research, Colonial Williamsburg, Inc., pp. 5-6.

54. Knight, (ed.), Documentary History of Education, I, 165-166.

to raise the extra £10 by a subscription in Williamsburg, but after his death Hunter asked that it be furnished out of the funds of the Associates.[55] Hunter also decided to accept only 24 scholars rather than the 30 which had been recommended. On Michaelmas, 1760, the Williamsburg school was able to begin operation.[56]

At their November 6, 1760 meeting the Associates approved the change in salary which Hunter had recommended for Mrs. Wager and followed another suggestion of his by asking Robert Carter Nicholas to become a trustee of the Williamsburg school in the place of Dawson. Then Hunter soon died, too; and the Rev. William Yates became a trustee.[57] At the death of Yates in 1764 the Rev. James Horrocks succeeded him as trustee, followed subsequently by Josiah Johnson and John Bracken.[58] It was the Treasurer of the colony, Nicholas, however, who served longest

---

55. Knight, (ed.), Documentary History of Education, I, 162.

56. Ibid., I, 165-166.

57. Ibid., I, 143-144.

58. Stephenson, "Notes on Negro School," p. 3.

and who became the most active trustee. His reports reached the Associates in London with considerable regularity; and, all in all, whatever success the Williamsburg school recorded owed much to his efforts.

Nicholas's first letter to the Associates was written on September 17, 1762. He had been to talk to Mrs. Wager, had looked into the condition of the school, and had decided matters stood about as they did at the time of Hunter's last report. But there is a tone of guarded pessimism in Nicholas's opinions, and he warned the Association that he had no "sanguine expectations" of the school's success.[59] However, the school apparently did very well over the next few years, and it was not long before Nicholas and Yates were writing that the students had "rather exceeded their Expectations."[60]

The minutes and correspondence of the Associates contain a clear picture of a number of phases of the operation of the school. It met, as William Hunter originally planned, in a house rented for both the school and living

---

59. Knight, (ed.), Documentary History of Education, I, 165-166.

60. Ibid., I, 152-153.

quarters for the teacher. The trustees, however, took
over responsibility for renting the building rather than
giving Mrs. Wager an extra allowance for that purpose.
From 1763 to 1765 they engaged a house owned by Dudley
Digges and possibly located on the northeast corner of
Henry and Ireland Streets, for which they paid £8 a year.
It proved too small, and in the latter part of 1765 the
school moved to a house of John Blair, for which the trustees agreed to pay £12 yearly. Here it remained until
its discontinuance.[61]

The best indication we have of the course of
study and the methods of teaching employed in the school
comes from the rules that Nicholas and Yates drew up in
1762 for the guidance of the schoolmistress.[62] She was
to take only scholars approved by the trustees, open the
school at seven o'clock in the winter and at six in the

---

61. Stephenson, "Notes on Negro School," p. 4,
App. I, citing Manuscripts of Dr. Bray's Associates, American Papers, 1735-1774, S.P.G. Archives, London.

62. Robert Carter Nicholas and William Yates to
[John Waring], September 30, 1762, Manuscripts of Dr. Bray's
Associates, American Papers, 1735-1774.

summer, enforce regular attendance, and keep her pupils "diligently to their Business during the Hours of Schooling." There were a number of rules governing religious instruction and worship: the teacher should see that her charges learned to read the Bible, she should catechize them according to the doctrines of the Church of England, she should take them to church regularly, and she should conduct prayers in the school. The teacher was also expected to insist upon personal cleanliness, neatness of dress, and moral behavior from the students. Finally, she was to "teach her Scholars the true Spelling of Names, make them mind their Stops & endeavour to bring them to pronounce & read distinctly." While the school thus laid a heavy emphasis on religion and to that extent resembled the simple classes sometimes conducted by the parish clergy, it is still clear from the emphasis on reading and writing and also from Nicholas's desire to require attendance for a minimum of three years that the intention was to provide a reasonable amount of formal academic training. The scholars, moreover, learned quite readily when left at school long enough, for Nicholas found that the ones who did remain for an adequate time were able "to read pretty well."[63] The trustees likewise appeared satisfied with Mrs. Wager's capabilities as a teacher.[64]

There seemed to be no difficulty in finding pupils for the school. At the request of the Associates Nicholas raised the enrollment of the school from 24 back to 30, and it remained close to, or a little above, that figure for the duration of the school.[65] The backers of the school never reported the same hostility to the idea of educating young slaves among residents of Williamsburg that they found among some planters who frankly expressed their fear of increasing the understanding of slaves.[66] Lists of the students and their masters survive for the years 1762, 1765, and 1769, the first of these also indicating the ages of the pupils. Most were 6 to 8 years of age, a few as young as 3, and one or two as old as 9

---

63. Knight, (ed.), Documentary History of Education, I, 159.

64. Ibid., I, 150, 156.

65. Ibid., I, 150, 158, 159.

66. Ibid., I, 152-153.

and 10. The masters who enrolled slaves in the school--
some thirty or more in these years--represent a good cross
section of political leaders like John Blair, Robert
Carter Nicholas, and John Randolph and of craftsmen, shop-
keepers, and innkeepers like Anthony Hay, Hugh Orr, Alexander Craig, and Jane Vobe. The College also enrolled
two of its slaves in 1769, and three of the children in
1762 and two in 1769 were free.[67]

Finances were never a major obstacle while the
Negro school was in operation except for the occasional
complaints of both Hunter and Nicholas at the high cost
of renting a school building. The Associates continued
to supply an annual payment of £30 toward the expenses
of the school, which was £10 more than they had originally planned, until their meeting of March 3, 1768,
when they voted to reduce their grant to £25.[68] Robert
Carter Nicholas promised in his letter of January 1, 1770,
that the people of Williamsburg would meet any additional

---

67. Stephenson, "Notes on Negro School," App. I,
pp. iii-iv.

68. Knight, (ed.), Documentary History of Education,
I, 162.

expense.[69] The treasurer mentioned in 1772 that "some few of the Inhabitants do join with him in contributing towards support of the School, tho' there is far from a general disposition to promote its success."[70] Additional expenses beyond the amount of the grant from the Associates would appear to have been very small. In the years when the trustees were paying £8 rent, they paid Mrs. Wager £28 yearly, making a total expenditure of £36, or £6 over the allotment received from England. After the rental of the larger house at £12, the teacher's salary apparently dropped to £20, making a slightly reduced expenditure of £32 yearly.[71]

The turnover in students remained the most persistent problem the school faced. The slaveowners in Williamsburg had been willing enough to send their slave children to classes, but in too many cases it turned out to be more for the benefit of a cheap nursery than out of more generous motives. As Nicholas reported:

---

69. Knight, (ed.), Documentary History of Education, I, 162.

70. Ibid., I, 164.

71. Stephenson, "Notes on Negro School," App. I, pp. i-ii.

> The Owners, as soon as the Children are able
> to do little offices about the House, either
> take them away from School entirely, or keep
> them from it at Times so that they attend
> only when there is no employment for Them at
> Home.[72]

Hence, he found few scholars remaining for the three years that he considered an absolute minimum.

A rather vague and mysterious problem arose in connection with enforcing the rules adopted for the school by the Associates. Robert Carter Nicholas spoke of these rules as a "very difficult Business" and mentioned the great need of delicacy in handling the situation, "however strange it may appear."[73]

There was a more comprehensible problem in the increasing age and infirmity of the teacher, Mrs. Wager. Nicholas always hoped to find a successor for her; but apparently he never could locate anyone as satisfactory. By December, 1771, the mistress' health was bad enough that she had lost considerable time from school.[74]

---

72. Knight, (ed.), Documentary History of Education, I, 159.

73. Ibid., I, 156.

74. Ibid., I, 163, 164.

Finally it was Mrs. Wager's death in 1774 that caused
the Williamsburg school to be closed.[75]

It has been charged that the expositions of
the catechism, testaments, psalters, sermons, and various guides for youth included were "entirely unfitted
for the people whom it was intended to benefit."[76] However, the list also included instruction books designed
for Indians, beginning English texts, and other works
which were probably the best available texts for the kind
of elementary instruction planned. It is difficult to
see what the Associates would have chosen, if not these.[77]

From time to time the Bray Associates tried to
support schools among the Negro population elsewhere in
Virginia. There was considerable correspondence back and
forth with two ministers in particular, the Rev. James
Marye of Orange County and the Rev. Jonathan Boucher of

---

75. Pennington, "Thomas Bray's Associates,"
pp. 360-361.

76. Goodwin, "Christianizing and Educating the
Negro," p. 152.

77. Minutes of Dr. Bray's Associates, Catalogue of
Books for Home and Foreign Libraries, Manuscripts of
Dr. Bray's Associates, S.P.G. Archives.

of Hanover and later Caroline County.[78] Both these men

received shipments of books for use among the large slave

populations of their parishes. Neither felt their par-

ishes were compact enough to support an organized school,

though Boucher occasionally employed educated Negroes to

teach,under his supervision, a few slaves in their own

neighborhood from books supplied by him.

Following the successful opening of the Williams-

burg school, the Associates hoped they might establish

two others at Norfolk and Yorktown.[79] However, no one

was willing to do the work that William Hunter and Robert

Carter Nicholas had performed in the capital, and no

school opened at either place. In Fredericksburg, in

which the Associates became interested on the advice of

Marye, Fielding Lewis undertook the establishment of a

school. Modeled closely on the one in Williamsburg and

using the rules Robert Carter Nicholas had prepared, it

opened in 1765 with 16 children. The scholars were all

---

78. Knight, (ed.), Documentary History of Education,
I, 144-149, 150, 154-157, 160-161.

79. Ibid., I, 149.

quite young, but Lewis was able to write that they "be-gin already to read prettily."[80]

The Fredericksburg school ran into precisely the same difficulty as the one at Williamsburg. The owners would not leave their young slaves enrolled long enough for adequate training. Lewis actually wanted to keep them five years, but he would have been happy to settle for two or three years.[81] Moreover, he ran into difficulty never encountered at Williamsburg of keeping the enrollment at a desired minimum. There were 17 scholars in 1766 but only 9 in the fall of 1768; and dur-ing the preceding summer regular attendance had dropped to 4. The few who did attend were learning to read well but were leaving school as soon as they had mastered this accomplishment.[82] After five years of operation Lewis closed the school because of the small attendance.[83]

---

80. Knight, (ed.), Documentary History of Educa-tion, I, 158-159.

81. Ibid., I, 160.

82. Ibid., I, 162.

83. Ibid., I, 163.

When all of the educational activities in Virginia of the Associates of Dr. Bray are added together, the sum comprises an honest and respectable effort. Yet it takes only a minute's reflection to realize how little their work affected the vast Negro population of eighteenth-century Virginia. A few young Negroes in Williamsburg, an even smaller number in Fredericksburg plus a few of the Negroes in maybe three or four rural parishes--these are not much more than the exceptions which prove the rule that educational opportunities for the Negro slaves were all but non-existent.

Yet, above all the other efforts the Negro school at Williamsburg stands out as a rather notable thing. Although the entire life of the school was not quite fifteen years, it was at the very least a moderate success. Classes operated at capacity even in the face of too brief an attendance from most of the scholars. If not always for the best motives, the masters displayed a willingness to have some of their young slaves educated at the school. What may be most significant of all is the indisputable fact that some of the scholars were learning to read and write, even under relatively adverse conditions. If nothing else, these young scholars had proved the slave's capacity for education.

4. The Negro and The Great Awakening

Beginning about the middle of the eighteenth century with the development of Presbyterianism and continuing on through the appearance of Methodists and Baptists, the religious revival known as the Great Awakening began to sweep through Virginia.[84] To some extent it was strongest in the western areas, where the Negro population was smallest; but these Protestant groups also developed a following in the Piedmont and coastal areas. It was not long before their evangelistic efforts embraced the Negroes; and ultimately, in the years following the Revolution, the churches that grew out of the Great Awakening won the loyalty of the overwhelming number of Christianized slaves.

---

84. The standard work is Wesley M. Gewehr, The Great Awakening in Virginia (Durham, N. C., 1930).

The conventional view has been that the missionary effort among the Negro slaves which was produced by the Great Awakening completely displaced the feebler Anglican efforts.[85] One Negro historian regarded the Great Awakening as the first real impulse for the conversion of the Negro.[86] Certainly there were many points which favored the new religious groups. Their clergy possessed a fervor and a drive that all too many ministers of the Established Church had lost. The form of worship in their churches included an emotional appeal that was more effective with many slaves. The requirements for baptism, turning more on an aroused religious feeling than an understanding of even the simplest catechism, were much easier for the average slave to satisfy. What also may have counted for much was the attitude of those slaveowners who were themselves converted in the Great Awakening. Far from opposing the baptism

---

85. Gewehr, Great Awakening in Virginia, p. 235, although note that on the basis of one letter Professor Gewehr makes the unwarranted implication that the Anglicans generally opposed baptizing slaves.

86. Luther P. Jackson, "Religious Development of the Negro in Virginia from 1760 to 1860," Journal of Negro History, XVI (April, 1931), 170-175.

of their slaves, they usually were inclined to encourage
it.[87] The Anglican parishes were also too disorganized
by the time of the Revolution to remain a real competitor.

Yet, in the period before the Revolution, it
is questionable whether the churches of the Great Awakening evidenced much more interest or achieved any greater success than had the Anglicans. The basic similarity,
in fact, in the approach to work among the slaves by the
Presbyterians, the first of the churches of the Great
Awakening to become active in Virginia, and by the Anglicans is far more striking than their differences.

Samuel Davies was one of the more successful
Presbyterian ministers in his appeals to slaves. In
1750 he wrote that he had baptized 40 Negroes in a year
and had a hundred among his congregation.[88] A few years
later he had a regular Negro following of perhaps 300,
of which about a third were baptized.[89] Yet large-scale

---

87. See, for example, "Journal of Col. James Gordon
of Lancaster County, Va.," William and Mary Quarterly, 1st
ser., XI (1902-1903), 108-112, 222-223.

88. Perry, Historical Collections, I, 369.

89. Gewehr, Great Awakening in Virginia, pp.235-236.

baptism of slaves was not unknown among Anglicans,
Jonathan Boucher had baptized 108 Negro children and 30
or 40 adults from the time of his arrival through 1762.[90]
Then on the Whitmonday holiday of 1767 he baptized 315.[91]
Davies and one or two other Presbyterian leaders were
also active in the operation of a school for Negroes,
largely supported by backers in London, that immediately
suggests a parallel with the schools of the Bray Associates.[92] Davies' own personal views on slavery thor-
oughly accorded with those of the vast majority of Anglican clergymen. Slavery, he held, did not destroy spir-
itual freedom; and conversion therefore did not require
the emancipation of slaves.[93]

This very real similarity between the position
of Samuel Davies and that of representative opinion among
Anglican clergymen should not obscure the fact that the

---

90. Knight, (ed.), Documentary History of Education,
I, 154-155.

91. Ibid., I, 160-161.

92. Earnest, Religious Development of the Negro in
Virginia, pp. 41-42.

93. Gewehr, Great Awakening in Virginia, pp. 236-237.

Established Church regarded the work of the Presbyterian leader with abhorrence.[94] Davies had published a small book, The Duty of Christians, dealing in very moderate terms with the obligation of masters to instruct their slaves in religion; and this publication became a particular object of attack.[95]

However, there were influences at work in the dissenting churches that led many of their followers to a more questioning attitude on slavery. Much of this development occurred after ideas about slavery had been colored by the natural rights philosophy of the Revolution. At that, none of the Great Awakening churches ever took a consistent stand against slavery. Of all the religious groups in Virginia before 1800 only the Quakers went that far. However, through the 1780's both the Baptists and Methodists were involved in controversies over slavery. The closest either came to an official condemnation of slaveholders was the declaration of 1784

---

94. Gewehr, Great Awakening in Virginia, pp. 85, 96.

95. William and Mary Quarterly, 2nd ser., I (October, 1921), 280-281.

requiring all Methodists in the United States to free
their slaves. This remained in force only one year and
was not even then effectively enforced.[96] But both
churches contained sizeable groups of ministers and lay-
men who manumitted their own slaves. Large slaveowners
such as the Baptists David Barrow and Robert Carter were
involved, as well as lesser owners like the group of
Methodists of Sussex County who manumitted nearly a hundred slaves at a single court session during the revival
of 1787-1788.[97]

After the Revolution the Methodists and Baptists, and to a lesser extent the Presbyterians, far out-
stripped the remnant of Episcopalians in work among the
Negroes. By 1790, when about one Negro in 23 in Virginia
was a church member, over 80% of them were Baptists and
Methodists.[98] Initially most of them became members of
predominantly white congregations under white leadership.

---

96. Gewehr, Great Awakening in Virginia, pp. 245-246.

97. Ibid., p. 249. See also Virginia Magazine, IV
(January, 1897), 281.

98. Jackson, "Religious Development of the Negro in
Virginia from 1760 to 1860," pp. 179-180.

Except for a few isolated cases, they sat in special sec-
tions of the church and had no real voice in congregational
affairs. In short, for all the supposed democratizing influences of the Great Awakening, there was no difference in
the status of these Negroes and those who had attended Anglican churches before the Revolution, except that somewhat more of them were baptized church members.

5. The Negro Baptist Church in Williamsburg

One development was taking place in the churches
of the Great Awakening that was eventually to be of great
consequence in the religious history of the Negro. By
the 1780's a number of Negro preachers had appeared who
were beginning to develop a devoted following among their
people. Among these were two itinerants, Lewis and Harry
Hosier, and also two men, one called Moses and the other
Gowan Pamphlet, through whom the Great Awakening made its
impact on the Negro community of Williamsburg.[99]

---

99. Jackson, "Religious Development of the Negro
in Virginia from 1760 to 1860," pp. 175-176.

The efforts of these two men, especially
Pamphlet, resulted in the establishment of a Negro Baptist Church in Williamsburg that was one of the earliest
all-Negro congregations in the United States. The claim
has sometimes been made that it was the first Negro
church in the country, but like so many "firsts" it is
not an easy matter to substantiate.[100] So much of the
information about this particular church is a well-blended
mixture of tradition and fact that it is difficult to
winnow out the true account of its establishment.[101]

Logically the church must have had its beginning in informal meetings at which Moses and Gowan
Pamphlet preached. The meetings may well have been secret, as Moses was frequently arrested and whipped for
holding them.[102] There is a tradition that the meetings

---

100. See Earnest, Religious Development of the Negro
in Virginia, p. 54, for an assertion that the Williamsburg
congregation was the first Negro church.

101. Probably the most reliable account is that in
Robert B. Semple, A History of the Rise and Progress of
Baptists in Virginia, a work almost contemporary with the
early Negro church here and one which went through many
nineteenth-century editions. The one of 1894, revised
and extended by G. W. Beale (Richmond, Va., 1894), has
been used in this report.

102. Ibid., p. 148.

began at Green Spring, then shifted to a spot known as Raccoon Chase, and then about 1776 began to take place in Williamsburg.[103]

By the time that Pamphlet had come from Middlesex County and begun to preach to the Williamsburg group, the Baptist leaders in the state had forbidden Negroes to do so. However, Pamphlet defied the church leadership by continuing to preach and to baptize with the result that, for a time, he was under a sentence of excommunication.

With the backing of his baptized followers, who seemed to number about 330, Pamphlet formed an organized church and became its pastor.[104] Even though it came at a time when the congregation and its pastor were out of favor with the white Baptists, this foundation under Pamphlet's leadership would appear to be the real beginning of the Williamsburg group as an organized church. There is some variation in impressions about the date of formation of Pamphlet's congregation. The present-day

---

103. See folder issued by First Baptist Church, Williamsburg, Va., copy in Colonial Williamsburg Archives.

104. Semple, History of Baptists, pp. 118-119, 148.

church claims the date 1776.[105] It has also been put at
1781 on the strength of a citation to Asplund's Register
for 1794; the date 1785 has also been given.[106] What
seems most likely is that the informal meetings of Negroes
may have begun around 1776 but that any formal organization of the congregation did not take place before the
1780's.

Despite its insurgent status the church pros-
pered over the next few years. Membership climbed to
around 500; and since the congregation included a number
of literate members, written church records were kept.[107]
Then, in 1791, peace was restored with the Virginia Baptists, when the congregation petitioned for admittance
into the Dover Association.[108] A meeting of the Association in Mathews County, which received the petition of

---

105. Folder issued by First Baptist Church, Williamsburg, Va., copy in Colonial Williamsburg Archives.

106. Jackson, "Religious Development of the Negro
in Virginia from 1760 to 1860," p. 189; Earnest, Religious Development of the Negro in Virginia, p. 54.

107. Semple, History of Baptists, p. 148.

108. Ibid.

Pamphlet's flock, appointed a group of visitors; and at the meeting of October 12, 1793, the Dover Association accepted the Williamsburg church into full membership.[109]

Within the next few years Gowan Pamphlet died, and the church was without a regular pastor.[110] The subsequent history of this congregation in the first two or three decades of the nineteenth century becomes difficult to establish. Sometime in those years Pamphlet's original church went out of existence, to be revived later as the First Baptist Church.[111] So, while the present-day Negro church claims direct descent from Pamphlet's group, there was a break in continuity. Likewise, the Negro church began in the nineteenth century, perhaps very early in it, to use the property on Nassau Street between Duke of Gloucester and Francis Streets, where the present-day First Baptist Church occupied an 1855 structure until its recent demolition.

What happened to Pamphlet's church and its successor in the nineteenth century need not concern us

---

109. Semple, History of Baptists, p. 126.

110. Ibid., pp. 118-119.

111. Ibid., p. 148n.

so much, however, as the circumstances under which this congregation was originally established. It was probably the first manifestation of the spirit of the Great Awakening in Williamsburg, and there seems no reason to deny it a place as at least one of the earliest Negro churches in the country. But Gowan Pamphlet's group has an additional significance that goes beyond the mere date of establishment; for, unlike many of the other early Negro churches, it was from the beginning an all-Negro congregation founded without white assistance and, in fact, in defiance of white control.[112]

---

112. The Petersburg and Norfolk churches, two of the other early Virginia Negro churches, developed out of congregations that were originally mixed. Jackson, "Religious Development of the Negro in Virginia from 1760 to 1860," pp. 189-190.

Chapter X

THE LAW AND THE NEGRO

1. Colonial Black Codes

The evolution of the Negro's legal status from
ordinary indentured servant to servant for life to slave
was followed by the development of a separate legal code,
distinct trial procedures, and harsher punishments for
Negroes accused of criminal acts. Inevitably the slave's
lack of personal freedom would have necessitated some revision in the English legal system that had been transported to Virginia. But it was unrelenting fear of the
Negro as a potential insurrectionist and constant determination to police his conduct rigidly that instigated
most of the early laws affecting Negro slaves.

Only in the last two decades of the seventeenth
century did anything more than the faintest beginning of
a separate criminal law for Negroes begin to appear. An
act of 1680 for preventing Negro insurrections was the
first real "black code" in Virginia, providing specific

punishments for the three crimes of leaving the master's property without permission; lifting a hand against a "Christian," that is, a white man; and for hiding or resisting capture after running away.[1] Conviction on the last charge required the death penalty. A 1691 statute that was of the greatest importance as the first legal restriction on manumission of slaves in Virginia also provided a systematic plan for raising a force of men to recapture "outlying slaves," or runaways who were in hiding.[2] Then in 1692 the legislature provided the first trial procedures, in particular the denial of jury trial, which applied specifically to Negro slaves.[3]

There were three more or less comprehensive pieces of legislation in the eighteenth century covering the trial, punishment, and regulation of slaves. The first passed in 1705 to be replaced in 1723 by one which was in turn superseded by the act of 1748.[4] These were

---

1. William Waller Hening, (ed.), The Statutes at Large Being a Collection of all the Laws of Virginia (Richmond, Va., etc., 1810-1823), II, 481-482.

2. Ibid., III, 86-88.

3. Ibid., III, 102-103.

4. Ibid., III, 447-462; IV, 126-134; VI, 104-112.

the basic codes for the later colonial period, and most
of the other legislation affecting Negro crimes, with
the exception of laws dealing with runaways, was not much
more than a minor modification of these two measures.

As has already been suggested, the first law
aimed at a crime by Negroes other than running away was
the 1680 statute designed to prevent insurrections by
punishing slaves who kept their master's property without permission or resisted a white man in any way.[5] On
the supposition that this act went unnoticed the Assembly
required two years later that it be read twice a year in
every church.[6] The more comprehensive statute of 1723
sought new safeguards against an armed rising by with-
drawing the privilege of benefit of clergy from Negroes
convicted of plotting or attempting such rebellion and
by forbidding all assemblies of slaves that were not licensed by the masters and held for public worship.[7] It
also denied all Negroes free or slave the right to possess

---

5. Hening, Statutes, II, 481-482.

6. Ibid., II, 492-493.

7. Ibid., IV, 126-134.

weapons, except that free Negroes who were householders or militiamen might keep a single gun and Negroes residing on the frontier might be licensed by the justice of the peace to carry arms.[8] All of these restrictions continued in force under the law of 1748.[9]

Most crimes other than running away or rising in rebellion that a Negro might commit were actions defined in laws that applied equally to all persons in the colony. It is revealing, however, that two felonies, hog stealing and the administration of poisonous medicines, were the occasion of special provisions dealing exclusively with slaves. Hog stealing reached the point that on the third conviction it became a capital offense without benefit of clergy.[10] Such were the risks involved in the temptations of the delicate flavor of roast pig.

The restriction of poisonous medicines obviously arose out of the belief of the whites that a great many Negroes continued to practice the witchcraft and

---

8. Hening, Statutes, IV, 126-134.

9. Ibid., VI, 104-112.

10. Ibid., VI, 122-123.

tribal medicine they had brought from Africa both in honest, if primitive, attempts to cure ailing slaves but also in malicious attempts to destroy an enemy. One section of the 1748 code provided capital punishment for Negroes who prepared and administered medicine of any sort, unless their owner had consented.[11] Benefit of clergy was allowable only where the slave could prove there had been no evil intent. In the wave of Negro crimes which David Mays described in Caroline County from 1761-1764 there were no less than three trials under this law in a three months period during 1762 with convictions in two of them.[12]

Beginning with the legislation of 1692 a separate court procedure developed for the trial of Negroes differing markedly in its rapid movement to trial and lack of constitutional guarantees from that accorded the free man. In capital cases the core of this process was (1) the immediate imprisonment of the slave, (2) issuance

---

11. Hening, Statutes, VI, 105.

12. David J. Mays, Edmund Pendleton, 1721-1803; A Biography (Cambridge, Mass., 1952), I, 42-44.

by the governor of a commission of oyer and terminer to
persons in the county involved to arraign and indict the
offender and to take for evidence the confession of the
accused or the oaths of two witnesses, or one in some
cases, and (3) "without the sollemnitie of jury" to pass
such judgment as the law allowed.[13] Throughout the colonial era there was but one modification in this method
of trial. In 1765 the governor was permitted to issue
general commissions of oyer and terminer to four or more
justices of the peace in each county, including one of
the quorum, thereby eliminating the necessity of a special commission for each trial.[14]

Initially the procedure for trying slaves did
not provide for testimony by other Negroes. In 1723,
however, it became permissible in capital cases involving Negroes to take such testimony from Negroes, Indians,
or mulattoes "as shall seem convincing," wording which
clearly implied that they were not to be accepted as
sworn witnesses nor to be questioned at all, except when

---

13. Hening, Statutes, III, 102-103.

14. Ibid., VIII, 136-139.

absolutely necessary.[15] However, this provision for the use of slave testimony in 1723 may have been an opening wedge for employing Negro witnesses far more widely than the law intended. For a new law of 1732 stated that no Negro, mulatto, or Indian should be admitted in court, be sworn as a witness, or give evidence in a case--practices which the law complained had been allowed, even in the General Court--except in the trial of a slave for a capital offense.[16] One subsequent modification occurred in 1748 when free Christian Negroes, Indians, and mulattoes were allowed to appear in any case involving another Negro, Indian, or mulatto.[17] In brief, however, all these technicalities come down to the fact that the slaves normally could testify only in a capital case involving another Negro.

After 1732 the Negro possessed some fragments of that medieval remnant, benefit of clergy, to soften the harsh processes of justice under which he was often

---

15. Hening, Statutes, IV, 127.

16. Ibid., IV, 326-327.

17. Ibid., VI, 107.

tried and convicted. This is not the place for a discussion of the long evolution of that institution from its origin as a means of protecting persons in clerical orders from trial in civil courts to the point that it saved all literate persons and finally virtually the entire population from certain punishments. To the Virginia Negro it was a means of escaping the prescribed punishment for his first commission of a good many capital crimes.[18] If his felony fell within benefit of clergy, the slave was burned in the hand to show that he had exhausted his use of the privilege. Then he received corporal punishment and was released.[19]

There is some question as to how early in the history of Virginia Negro slaves were able to claim benefit of clergy. Dalzell's study regards the 1732 law regulating the pleading of this privilege by Negroes as both the first regulation of benefit of clergy in the laws of the colony and the first occasion of its extension

---

18. An excellent discussion is George W. Dalzell, Benefit of Clergy in America & Related Matters (Winston-Salem, N. C., 1955), Ch. X.

19. Hening, Statutes, IV, 326.

to slaves.[20]   However, there was an earlier law in 1723
which placed insurrection or murder by a slave outside
the privileges of benefit of clergy, an indication that
Negroes might already have been clergyable.[21]

But Dalzell was probably entirely correct in
thinking there was a considerable area of doubt about
how far benefit of clergy extended to Negro slaves, and
even to other Virginians. In particular the laws of
England had not allowed women and persons who were illit-
erate to claim benefit of clergy until the reigns of
William and Mary and Anne. It was not at all certain
that these acts applied in the colonies to anyone. Moreover, the laws affecting the baptism of Negroes had not
considered the possibility that conversion to Christianity
conferred the right to benefit of clergy on slaves.

The 1732 legislation was the direct outgrowth
of a case involving a Negro slave in which many of these
doubts were combined. Mary Aggie, Virginia-born, Christianized, and the property of a Williamsburg widow, had

---

20. Dalzell, _Benefit of Clergy_, pp. 99, 104.

21. Hening, _Statutes_, IV, 126.

committed a larceny for which she would have been clergyable in England, if a free woman. Governor Gooch interested himself in the case for some unexplained reason
and after Mary Aggie's conviction by the Commission of
Oyer and Terminer for York County, had an application for
benefit of clergy entered in her behalf. The case was
eventually considered by the Council and the General Court,
and then submitted to England for a ruling. At that point
all evidence of the outcome disappears, but then in 1732
the Virginia Assembly passed laws affecting benefit of
clergy for women, illiterates, and slaves.[22]

Further definitions of benefit of clergy for
slaves usually took the form of placing certain felonies
outside the plea of clergy. Insurrection or murder fell
beyond its scope in 1723.[23] Manslaughter, felonious
breaking and entering, and thefts involving more than
five shillings were exempted in 1732.[24] Then it was

---

22. Mary Aggie's case is summarized in Dalzell,
Benefit of Clergy, pp. 99-104; the 1732 statute is in
Hening, Statutes, IV, 326.

23. Hening, Statutes, IV, 126.

24. Ibid., IV, 326.

denied for a third conviction for hog stealing and for
the malicious administration of poisonous medicines by
the laws of 1748.[25] So, in effect, so far as slaves were
concerned the privilege of benefit of clergy began gradually to contract, except that in 1772 there was one re-
definition of its applicability in cases of breaking and
entering that favored the accused.[26]

Cases in which a Negro was on trial for a felony usually came to the courts with a minimum of delay.[27]
The special commissions of oyer and terminer helped speed
the process, but efficiency was less at issue than the
desire to impress other Negroes with the swift course of
justice. In the long run a speedy trial was in the Negro's
best interest, for slaves who did languish in jail awaiting trial sometimes paid a heavy penalty in physical suf-
fering before they could begin to pay for their crime. In
its 1762 session, for instance, the Burgesses noted an
allowance of £3:15:0 to a Caroline County man to compensate him for loss of thirty days labor by a slave who had

---

25. Hening, Statutes, VI, 105, 122-123.

26. Ibid., VIII, 522-523.

27. Mays, Edmund Pendleton, I, 45-46.

been frostbitten while confined. That same session it
had to allow £80 to the owner of a slave who had lost
both his legs and finally died from the frostbite he suffered in a cold jail.[28]

Peter Hansborough of Stafford County petitioned
the Burgesses in an even worse case in 1771, but the delegates did not seem much disposed to compensate Hansborough
for the death of his slave Sharper. The Negro had been
charged with administering medicine illegally and was im-
prisoned to await examination by the justices. The weather
turned so cold and rainy that, while Hansborough made his
appearance at court, the justices declined to attend.
Hansborough inquired after his slave and "found he was
bitt by the Frost to Such a Degree that it Commanded Pity
from every human heart." This was December, and the trial
dragged on until May, when Sharper was acquitted. Hansborough related that he then "took the Poor distressed
Slave home...[where he]...died."[29]

28. John P. Kennedy, (ed.), Journals of the House
of Burgesses of Virginia, 1761-1765 (Richmond, Va., 1907),
pp. 71, 97, 102, 119.

29. Virginia Magazine of History and Biography, XVIII
(October, 1910), 394-396.

Just as the very nature of slave status had demanded trial procedures that to some extent abridged the traditional English and colonial guarantees of individual right, it just as logically required a system of punishment that was exclusively corporal. The courts might fine a master whose neglect contributed in some way to a criminal act of one of his Negroes, but the slave could not normally make satisfaction in this way. For minor offenses or when the slave was able to avail himself of benefit of clergy, whipping became the prescribed penalty--10 lashes for coming on a plantation without permission, 39 lashes for attending an unlawful meeting, or 39 for possessing weapons illegally, to cite a few examples.[30]

More serious crimes which did not warrant capital punishment, even in the harsh criminal codes of the day, required what may have been a more unpleasant fate than death itself. That penalty was mutilation or dismemberment. A slave giving false evidence would, for

---

30. Hening, Statutes, II, 481-482; III, 179; IV, 126-134; etc. Corporal punishment of this sort could be ordered by a single justice in many instances. See Mays, Edmund Pendleton, I, 45.

instance, receive his 39 lashes and then have his ears
nailed to the pillory for half an hour, after which
they would be cut off.[31] Under the law of 1748 his ears
would have been nailed to the pillory and then cut off
one at a time rather than simultaneously.[32] Dismemberment was a favorite punishment for the slave who continually ran away, went abroad at night, or lay in hiding.
Both the 1723 and 1748 acts specify its use for these
offenses. Since the dismemberment usually took the form
of cutting off a foot, it was a practical, if cruel, way
of curbing the sort of ungovernable Negro who really constituted the greatest threat of all against slavery as a
police institution. That dismemberment sometimes reached
proportions which struck even slaveowners as barbarous is,
however, evidenced by a 1769 statute which in the future
forbade the castration of a slave for continually lying
out and reserved that punishment solely for Negroes
guilty of the attempted rape of a white woman.[33]

---

31. Hening, Statutes, IV, 127.

32. Ibid., VI, 106-107.

33. Ibid., VIII, 358.

Finally there were the whole series of crimes for which conviction carried the death penalty, the felonies for which white persons would also have been executed plus offenses such as rebellion or the administering of medicines that applied only to slaves. According to the customary practice of colonial Virginia slaves were ordinarily hanged, but a slave named Eve who was convicted in Orange County of poisoning her master was drawn upon a hurdle to the place of execution and there burned at the stake.[34] Then there are also instances in which the head of a slave who had been hanged was cut off and put on public exhibition.

One economic problem arose with capital punishment of a slave. The owner was apt to view the execution as costing him the loss of a valuable piece of property, no matter how serious the slave's crime had been. In the 1705 statute affecting trial procedure for capital offenses, the justices were impowered to put a reasonable valuation upon any slave they condemned. When this valuation had been certified to the Assembly, the

---

34. Virginia Magazine, III (January, 1896), 308-310.

owner would be reimbursed from public funds.[35] This method of compensation remained in force throughout the colonial period with the result that few sessions of the Assembly fail to record favorable action on the request of some owner to be paid for an executed slave.[36]

The punishment which the courts meted out to slaves for crimes against public order in no way interfered with the disciplining of slaves by their owners and overseers. In fact, the law protected to extreme limits the master's privilege of punishing his slaves. One of the earliest pieces of legislation affecting slavery was the 1669 statute exempting a master from indictment for felony if a slave were killed while under punishment.[37] The law reasoned that there could be no felony without malicious intent and that no one could be presumed to destroy his own property deliberately and maliciously. The Assembly made some dent in this line

---

35. Hening, Statutes, III, 461.

36. A good example is Virginia Magazine, XVIII (July, 1910), 282-283.

37. Hening, Statutes, II, 270.

of reasoning in 1723, by providing that the master might be indicted if there were at least one lawful witness to testify that the killing of the slave had been a willful act.[38] But with this one unlikely exception owners remained exempt from prosecution for the death of a slave under correction, even though new royal governors were often instructed to work for laws to punish masters who deliberately killed or maimed a slave.

The dissection of a long list of laws is a tedious business at best; and once their contents have been outlined, there is not much more to be said. One significant development in the eighteenth century, however, was the collection of most of the criminal law affecting Negroes into the two comprehensive statutes of 1723 and 1748. They provided the colony with a "black code" nearly as well-defined and systematic as those of a later day.

This much can be said for the justice administered under these laws--it was often harsh, but it was uniform and not arbitrary. And it was rapid, for the

---

38. Hening, Statutes, IV, 132-133.

slave did not often languish in jail awaiting trial.
To that extent the slaves of colonial Virginia could
have fared worse, as indeed they did in parts of the
New World.

The net effect of these statutes, however, was
to make the law for the Negro slave almost exclusively a
police instrument for maintaining the stability of society and largely to demolish that more attractive side of
law, the safeguarding of the individual from unnecessary invasions of his person. Perhaps only the un-
comfortable fact that the slave was not fully a person
in the eyes of the law saved this one-sidedness from
seriously damaging, for free men even, the traditional
guarantees to the individual that Virginia had inher-
ited from English law.

2. The Incidence of Crime

The amount of legislative activity that went
into the establishment of a criminal law for Negroes
would imply a high rate of crime among slaves, but it is
largely impossible either to substantiate or to disprove

such an inference. The law may have been no more than
an expression of the white man's fear of what could hap-
pen rather than what actually happened. There is simply
not enough evidence to determine accurately the amount
of crime among slaves in the colonial period. Existing
studies have quickly abandoned any such effort.[39]

Ordinarily the more serious crimes that came
to trial by justices sitting under a special Commission
of Oyer and Terminer were not particularly frequent. In
the thirty-five year period from 1737 to 1772 Orange
County had 25 such trials involving 31 Negroes. Chester-
field County from 1749 to 1774, a period of twenty-five
years, witnessed 33 trials in which 44 Negroes were involved.[40]

There were more serious outbreaks of slave
crime once in a while, when the trials of Negroes for
felonies rose sharply. One of the best documented of these
crime waves, which David J. Mays has described quite fully,
swept through Caroline County in the three or four years

---

39. See, for example, Arthur P. Scott, _Criminal
Law in Colonial Virginia_ (Chicago, 1930), p. 311.

40. _Ibid._, p. 312.

at the end of the French and Indian War.[41] In a matter
of relatively few months no less than 12 Negroes went on
trial for various felonies, including murder, the illegal
administration of medicine, and arson. Nine of the twelve
were convicted and executed, two were allowed to plead
benefit of clergy, and only one won acquittal.[42]

Next to their consuming dread of an organized
slave rising the average white planter most feared an individual act of violence by one of his slaves. Poisoning
seemed to occupy a special niche in his chamber of horrors.
There were just enough instances of masters who had been
killed by a slave in this way to lend a certain amount of
justification to the whites' perpetual sense of insecurity.
In an age when no one could accuse the press of sensation-
alism a colonial printer never missed an opportunity to
report the poisoning of a master or overseer.[43]

The instances in which slaves were made to suf-
fer some indignity beyond the normal execution by hanging

---

41. Mays, Edmund Pendleton, I, 41.

42. Ibid., I, 42-44.

43. Georgia Gazette, March 30, 1768, which contains
an account of a multiple poisoning in Alexandria, Virginia.

were usually punishments for the murder of the Negro's master. The slave Eve who was burned at the stake in Orange County had poisoned her owner.[44] Most of the instances in which executed Negroes were to have their heads cut off and publicly displayed involved crimes of arson or poisoning.[45]

Since the courts did not often deal with petty crimes committed by slaves, it is even more difficult to say anything about such misdemeanors than about felonies which came to trial. The theft of a small article, a fight between two of the slaves, or some similar misdeed could be punished by the master without bringing the matter to the county court.[46]

Information about Negro crime in Williamsburg is as sketchy as that for the rest of the colony. There are enough newspaper accounts to assure that there were criminals among the slaves who lived here, if any such assurance were needed. And the range of their misdeeds

---

44. Virginia Magazine, III (January, 1896), 308.

45. Ibid., XVI (July, 1908), 95.

46. Scott, Criminal Law in Virginia, p. 311.

seems about what it was everywhere else. If anything,
there is a strong suggestion that, just as the slaves
of the capital were among the most skilled in the entire
colony, they also made the most artful criminals.

The annals of identifiable slave crimes in
Williamsburg begin with a mulatto slave, Sarah, the property of Archibald Blair, who received a death sentence
in 1728 for setting a house on fire.[47] Another account
of an equally grave felony concerns an attempted poisoning which was reported in the Maryland Gazette:

> WILLIAMSBURG. May 20, A Negro Boy in this
> City, set on by a Couple of Negro Fellows,
> went in his Mistress's Name to a Shop for
> some Arsenick to Poison Rats, and got a little;
> but took the Opportunity, when some Milk and
> Rice was on the Fire, to drop the Whole amongst
> it, unperceived: All the Family, consisting of
> nine or ten Persons, eat of it at Dinner, and
> in a few Minutes after were taken with a vio-
> lent Vomiting; which created a Suspicion of
> Poison being the Occasion, Physicians were im-
> mediately called, who ordered them what is
> necessary in those Cases, and it is hoped are
> now out of Danger. All the Negroes are taken
> up and committed to Prison, and it is hoped
> will be made Examples of, to deter others from
> such Villainy.[48]

---

47. York County Records, Orders and Wills, Book 16,
p. 511.

48. June 9, 1763.

Robbery appears to have been more common. A great many of the runaways from Williamsburg were Negroes who had fled after committing some theft.[49] John Greenhow observed of one of his runaways, a cooper named Harry, "He is a sly thief, few locks or doors will turn him, and is seldom long in a place before he puts his ingenuity in practice."[50] One instance of stealing by a free Negro is that of Charles Oats who broke into a cellar and took a chest of clothes and £50 cash.[51] Oats confessed, delivered up the money and part of the clothes, but then escaped. A slave named Moody was suspected in 1772 of having broken open an outhouse of Lord Dunmore's and made off with 19 turkeys belonging to the governor.[52] This was not the end of trouble for Moody, for the next year Benjamin Bucktrout advertised the slave's latest round of crimes:

> Run away a Negro Fellow, named Moody,
> a notorious Villain, who has been tried

---

49. Virginia Gazette, March 20, 1752.

50. Ibid., (Purdie), April 11, 1766.

51. Ibid., (Purdie), August 16, 1776.

52. Ibid., (Rind), March 26, 1772.

three Times at <u>York</u> Court, about three Weeks
ago he received a very serious Whipping for
knocking out a Negro's Eye, and last <u>Sunday</u>
robbed a white Man of twenty Shillings, and
a Silk Handkerchief. This is to forewarn
all Persons from harbouring or employing
him on any Account.[53]

John Greenhow seems to have had more than his share of dif-

ficulties over the crimes of his slaves. Harry, the sly

lock-picker, was an easy case compared with two other of

his Negroes, Fay and Emanuel. The first of the pair had

beaten his overseer, and Emanuel had fought with Greenhow

himself, throwing his master to the ground. The two, whom

Greenhow termed notorious thieves, then made their escape.[54]

3. The Fugitive Slaves

Much of the crime committed by Negro slaves was

to some degree one possible means of resisting the demands

of slavery. It was, to be sure, a fairly desperate method,

particularly if a slave resorted to anything so extreme

as the murder of his master and so insured his own execu-

tion. There was a much safer way of refusing to accept

---

53. <u>Virginia Gazette</u> (Purdie and Dixon), September 23, 1773.

54. <u>Ibid</u>., (Purdie), January 17, 1777.

bondage. That was simply to run away at the first opportunity. The chances of being retaken were good, but not
good enough to deter great numbers of slaves from becoming fugitives.

For a slave to run away was as much a criminal
act as for one to rob or kill. The owner did not have
to rely solely on his own resources to recapture his man.
He could count upon the machinery of law to assist him.
The fugitive slave represented in a number of ways, however, a distinct problem from the ordinary slave criminal.
His offense was too common to treat it as a felony, until
it became habitual.[55] Ordinarily he stood convicted by
his very act of flight; therefore provision for trial
and punishment by the courts were largely unnecessary.
Swift recapture and return to his owner were the basic
needs, and these the law tried to provide. Punishment
by whipping could be administered by the officials responsible for his return without a court decree.

---

55. For slaves who became habitual runaways or remained in hiding committing various depredations--"lying
out" as the eighteenth century expressed it--more drastic
legal procedures evolved. Two justices of the peace
could issue a proclamation permitting such offenders to
be killed without quarter. The sheriff could collect a

Prior to the advent of slavery in a legal sense Negroes were dealt with under the laws that applied to all runaway indentured servants, white or black. These enactments required fugitives to serve extra time, usually twice the length of their absence, as compensation to the master for the loss of their labor.[56] It was, in fact, a revision of these laws that constituted the first legal recognition in Virginia that the status of the Negro was changing so that he could be held as a servant for life. This occurred in the statute of 1661/62 which referred specifically to "negroes who are incapable of making satisfaction by addition of time."[57]

Not much later, in 1669, a system by which recaptured servants were to be returned to their masters was defined by law. A fugitive who was retaken was carried before the nearest justice in order to determine

---

force to hunt them down, or an individual captor might collect a reward for killing a Negro outlawed in this manner. If an "outlying" slave were taken alive, he was not executed, however, but punished by dismemberment. Hening, Statutes, III, 86, 210-211, 460-461; IV, 32; VI, 110-111; VIII, 358, 522-523.

56. Ibid., I, 254-255, 401, 440.

57. Ibid., II, 116-117.

the name of his master. Then the man was to be delivered
from constable to constable along the route to his home.[58]
The next year the law was modified to instruct each constable to give the fugitive a severe whipping as he passed
through his jurisdiction, and at the same time runaway
Negroes were specifically stated to be comprehended in
these acts.[59] A reward was also established for recapturing a runaway--1,000 pounds of tobacco in 1669 but reduced in 1670 to a less attractive 200 pounds with much
more stringent inquiry into the claimant's right to collect.[60]

    After slavery was fully established, these ar-
rangements, that is, the reward of 200 pounds of tobacco
and the system of returning runaways through successive
constables remained in force with only minor variations.
Thus the 1705 law, while largely repeating existing regulations, did omit the requirement that every constable
through whom a man was returned should administer a

---

58. Hening, Statutes, II, 273-274.

59. Ibid., II, 277-279.

60. Ibid., II, 283-284.

whipping.[61] Now only the first constable gave his thirty-nine lashes; so a hapless fugitive might have gotten home with at least a little skin on his back.

The 1705 law also introduced another modification in which the Public Gaol at Williamsburg figured prominently. Before it had been more or less assumed that the recaptured man would identify the name and residence of his owner. The Assembly overlooked the growing number of Negroes, some of whom knew no English and could not give this information and others of whom pretended to be new and feigned a lack of understanding of English. Now, when it was impossible to identify the owner, a slave was to be brought down to Williamsburg to the Public Gaol of the colony.[62] Eventually it became permissible to sell Negroes unclaimed after a reasonable time. With the founding of a newspaper in Williamsburg, it also became possible for the jailer to advertise runaways he was holding.

Justices and constables immediately began to send unidentified runaways to the capital, at times in

---

61. Hening, Statutes, III, 456-457.

62. Ibid., III, 456.

such haste that a slave taken only a few miles from his home plantation might well be sent a long distance to Williamsburg before anyone had a chance to identify him. So, after 1726, it was necessary to hold a Negro first for two months in the jail of the county where he had been captured. Then if he had not been claimed, the constable would pass him along through the other constables to the Public Gaol.[63] The volume of Negroes brought to Williamsburg under these laws was considerable, for the columns of the Virginia Gazette carried a more or less steady flow of advertisements.[64] Such runaways may have furnished an addition to the local labor force, since they could be hired out under proper safeguards. Not many of the unidentified ones were sold here, since the court of the county in which they had first been captured had this authority.

In 1748, the same year in which the main body of criminal law affecting Negroes was overhauled and consolidated, an attempt was made to do the same thing

---

63. Hening, Statutes, IV, 168-175.

64. See, for example, Virginia Gazette, September 15, 1737; September 22, 1738; March 21, 1745; January 2, 1752.

regarding runaways in an act on servants and slaves.[65]
This latter enactment, however, failed to include a sus-
pending clause, holding up its effective date until it
had received the royal assent. For this reason Virginians
received notice in 1752 that it had been disallowed, but
the Assembly moved quickly to pass a similar law in the
proper form in 1753.[66] It was essentially a restatement
of the law as it had stood since 1726.

In the 1760's there was a final attempt to alter the means of handling captured fugitives. An act of
1765 provided for a captor who had determined the owner
of a fugitive to carry the man before the justice of the
peace of the county. Then the captor was to take the responsibility of returning the runaway to the master upon
himself, for which he was entitled to payment of 5 shillings plus 4 pence a mile.[67] This method, while eliminating the use of the constables except for slaves whose
masters could not be determined, had obvious shortcomings.

---

65. Hening, Statutes, V, 547-548.

66. Ibid., VI, 356-369.

67. Ibid., VIII, 135-137.

It is no surprise to find the law altered four years later in 1769 on the ground that it had been ineffective. Now a captor could follow the procedure of 1765, receiving larger sums of 10 shillings plus 6 pence a mile; or he could simply take the runaway to the county jail, where the older arrangements that still applied to slaves of unidentified masters could be followed.[68]

The conclusion is inescapable that the volume of runaway slaves was large, large enough to sap a part of the economic advantage of a slave labor force. The small stereotype of a black figure hurrying along with a parcel of clothing tied on a stick and slung across his shoulder identified listings of fugitives in substantially every issue of the Gazette. From George Washington to the humblest master few owners escaped the loss of Negroes in this way.[69]

The ease with which the slave community in Williamsburg hid fugitives must suggest that the capital

---

68. Hening, Statutes, VIII, 358-361.

69. The Negro in Virginia. Compiled by the Writers' Program of the Work Projects Administration (New York, 1940), p. 128.

was no more immune from runaways than anywhere else in the colony and that recapturing them was no easier. Its share of the Gazette advertisements was large, and not even the printers themselves escaped the disagreeable necessity of using their own columns to attempt to recover a slave.[70]

Not all of these escaped slaves had an idea of achieving permanent freedom. Free soil did not yet exist to the north. If a slave really intended to live as a free man, the possibilities were limited and, in some cases, the hardships almost as unendurable as slavery itself. He had essentially two alternatives. He might make his way to one of the hidden, illegal communities of refugee Negroes on the western frontier of Virginia or in the Dismal Swamp. Otherwise and with less risk, if he were a skilled craftsman or light-skinned, he might get to a settled community where he could pass without too many questions as a free Negro. For Virginia slaves in the eighteenth century North Carolina offered the best opportunity for this latter course.

---

70. Virginia Gazette (Purdie and Dixon), November 24, 1768; (Dixon and Hunter), January 28, 1775; (Purdie), March 8, 1776.

Bob, a slave of the Williamsburg innkeeper, William Trebell, is a good illustration.[71] Bob, a man of 26 described as having been "burnt when young, by which he has a scar on the wrist of his right hand, the thumb of his left hand burnt off, and the hand [turned] in," escaped on a Saturday night in April of 1767. It is his past which was, however, more relevant. Bob had just been brought back from Hertford County in North Carolina after being away eight years. Part of the time he had lived in Charleston, South Carolina. Then for the last three years he had lived in North Carolina under the name of Edward or Edmund Tamar, had married, and with the protection of a man named Van Pelt had passed as a freeman. The fact that he could read and write and was an able carpenter and tailor had certainly made his deception easier. Some of the Negro women in Williamsburg were also able to get away in the hope of passing as free, including Nanny, "a brisk genteel sensible wench,"

---

71. *Virginia Gazette* (Purdie and Dixon), April 16, 1767. See also the advertisement by James Southall for his slave, Peter, *ibid*., (Purdie and Dixon), January 8, 1767.

whom her owner, Jane Vobe, suspected of having gone off with the New American Company of actors.[72]

Very frequently runaway slaves were less concerned about a permanent escape than simply returning to a locale from which they had recently been purchased or moved. John Maclean, for instance, bought a slave girl, Judith, and her year-old child at the sale of slaves from Middlesex County held on April 30, 1773, at Williamsburg. The following day she slipped off and was advertised as having probably started back to her Middlesex master.[73] Another girl, only 14 or 15 years old, from this same lot of slaves escaped in October, presumably to return to her mother, who was still a cook for the planter who had sold the daughter.[74] John, "6 feet high, 17 years old, well grown, with remarkable long feet," was known to have returned from Williamsburg to Warwick, where he had a father and some other relatives.[75] Often the

---

72. Virginia Gazette (Purdie and Dixon), June 30, 1768.

73. Ibid., (Purdie and Dixon), May 6, 1773.

74. Ibid., (Purdie and Dixon), January 27, 1774.

75. Ibid., (Purdie), July 25, 1777.

attraction of the slave's former residence was the fact
that a wife or husband was still living there, as in the
case of Peter, the property of John Fox of Williamsburg,
who for this reason had returned to Gloucester County.[76]
Running away for the sake of returning to a familiar location or rejoining relatives was a two-way street so far
as Williamsburg was concerned; for there were also slaves
who escaped into town after being sold or leased elsewhere. One instance of this is the case of Billy, a 20-
year old slave advertised by his master in Amherst County
as a runaway and suspected of having gone back to Williamsburg, since he had grown up and been trained as a
shoemaker there.[77] In a number of instances slaves who
had accompanied masters to Williamsburg took advantage
of the busy atmosphere of the capital to make an escape.[78]

   After a time it becomes distinctly noticeable
how many runaway Negroes were drawn from the more highly

76. Virginia Gazette (Purdie), October 17, 1777.

77. Ibid., (Clarkson and Davis), October 30, 1779.

78. Ibid., (Purdie and Dixon), March 31, 1768;
June 29, 1769; November 14, 1771.

skilled classes of labor. A high proportion seemed to be craftsmen, and some were able to read and write. The average runaway often seemed to be a slave like Johnny, a mulatto serving man, able to read and write, and once the property of Peyton Randolph, who escaped from Edmund Randolph in late 1777.[79]

It cannot be overlooked, however, that many runaway slaves were simply ordinary field hands, quite often so recently imported that they knew no English. This was more characteristic of the early eighteenth century and of other areas than Williamsburg, although most of the recaptured slaves brought into the Public Gaol, because their masters were unidentified, were "new Negroes."[80] There was one occasion when a group of fourteen recently imported Negroes fled in a body from a Hanover County merchant, John Burnley, who was probably holding them for sale.[81]

---

79. Virginia Gazette (Purdie), December 12, 1777.

80. Ibid., September 2, 1737; September 15, 1737; September 28, 1738; January 2, 1752; (Purdie and Dixon), July 8, 1773; February 3, 1774; June 16, 1774; August 4, 1774.

81. Ibid., (Purdie and Dixon), August 19, 1773. Two months later Burnley had recovered ten of the Negroes,

In the final analysis these runaways were perhaps a mixed lot, as mixed as their motives for escape. Some had genuine hopes of freedom, and a very few made good on them. Some fled from sheer desperation, not caring any longer about the risk of recapture. Others were more temporary absentees than real fugitives, seeking only a brief return to relatives from whom they had been separated. Whatever the reasons, the number of slaves who, in the eighteenth century use of the word, "eloped" is a powerful argument that few Negroes accepted the demands of slavery complacently.

4. The Threat of Rebellion

There has already been occasion, in connection with the movement for high import duties on slaves, to comment on the lurking fear of insurrection which haunted every slaveowner. As the number of slaves mounted steadily toward half the population of the colony--and, of course, more than half in areas where the slaves were really concentrated--it became possible to conceive of

---

but the others were still in hiding near West Point. Ibid., (Purdie and Dixon), October 28, 1773.

the destruction of society itself, if a Negro uprising
were really to take hold. Newspapers all over the colonies were quick to publish every available detail of a
real or rumored attempt of slaves to rebel; and much of
the restrictive legislation against Negroes in the colony was admittedly aimed at this unwelcome possibility.[82]

To what extent was the alarm of the whites ex-
aggerated? One count of uprisings or threats of uprisings during the entire course of slavery in Virginia
lists 72 of which only 9 occurred before 1776.[83] The
truth is difficult to measure; for instead of specific,
brief episodes more often there were periods of general
unrest lasting several years at a time. Judged on this
basis, about a fourth of the years from 1700 to 1775 were
marred by an abnormal degree of this uneasiness. The
fact remains, however, that no white person was killed
in an organized slave insurrection in Virginia before
the Nat Turner rising of 1831.

---

82. The pertinent Virginia laws are those of 1680,
1682, 1723, and 1748. See above, section 1 of this chapter.

83. Negro in Virginia, p. 175.

The first recorded attempt at a slave uprising
in Virginia occurred in the Northern Neck in 1687. As
so often happened, one of the men involved confessed and
the attempt was checked. The slave who had been leader
was not executed but was whipped around Jamestown from
the prison to the gallows and back, forced to wear an
iron collar for the rest of his life, and forbidden ever
to leave his master's plantation.[84]

A more serious plot, which centered in Surry
and Isle of Wight Counties but also involved James City,
was uncovered in March, 1709.[85] Once again it was a
slave who betrayed the plan to the whites--a Negro named
Will, the property of Robert Ruffin of Surry.[86] It fell
to the Governor's Council to direct an investigation of
the whole matter and issue instructions for the trial
and punishment of the Negroes involved. The way in which

---

84. Negro in Virginia, p. 174; "Randolph Manuscript,"
Virginia Magazine, XIX (April, 1911), 151.

85. H. R. McIlwaine and Wilmer L. Hall, (eds.),
Executive Journals of the Council of Colonial Virginia
(Richmond, Va., 1925-1945), III, 234-235.

86. Journals of the House of Burgesses, 1702-1712,
p. 270.

they proceeded provides a good picture of the operation
of all levels of government in the colony in the face of
what, to these men, presented a serious crisis. First
of all, the Council apparently issued warrants for the
arrest of all suspects, similar to one issued for four
Negroes in Bruton Parish, Angola Peter, Bumbara Peter,
Mingo, and Robin.[87] Then the county justices of Surry
and Isle of Wight were ordered to examine all suspected
slaves, releasing those only slightly involved with
appropriate punishment and holding the leaders in the
county jail, until the record of their examination
could be examined by the President of the Council, Edmund
Jenings.[88] James City Negroes were not considered to be
so deeply involved. Here, with a single exception, the
slaves, who had been rounded up and held under guard,
were to be tried at the next county court, punished, and
released.[89] There is an account of the close cross examination of several of these slaves in a letter from

---

87. Virginia Magazine, XVII (January, 1909), 34.

88. Executive Journals of Colonial Virginia, III,
234-235.

89. Ibid., III, 235.

Philip Ludwell to Jenings. The questioning by Ludwell
and three others had cleared Commissary Blair's slaves
and a number of others of complicity, but it had also
turned up the evidence against John Brodnax's Jamy, the
one James City slave ordered held in prison.[90]

About a month later the Council ordered the
principal culprits, those still held in jail, to be tried
before the General Court, where three of them were presumably convicted and hanged. One of the "chief Actors,"
Peter, belonging to Samuel Thompson of Surry, had escaped, and a reward of £10 alive or £5 dead was offered
for his recapture.[91]

The episode had a happier ending for Robert
Ruffin's Will. After he had given away the insurrection,
it became necessary to move him to the Northern Neck because some of the other Negroes threatened his life.
Then at its meeting in the fall of 1710 the Assembly
voted him his freedom as a reward for his service to the

---

90. *Virginia Magazine*, XIX (January, 1911), 23-24.

91. *Executive Journals of Colonial Virginia*, III,
236; *Negro in Virginia*, p. 174.

colony, the occasion being marred only by the complaint
of his former master, Ruffin, that the £40 voted by the
Assembly was less than he had been offered for the Negro
by a prospective buyer.[92]

Another plan for an uprising was headed off in
1722, prompting Governor Drysdale to include in his first
message to the Assembly a request for improving the militia and for passing stricter laws as a protection against
Negroes.[93] The slave code was, in fact, strengthened
that year.[94]

The years of 1729 and 1730 seem to have brought
a relatively longer period of unrest among slaves which
may have continued through most of the decade of the
30's.[95] The first incident occurred in June of 1729 on
a new plantation near the head of the James River. There
a group of about fifteen Negroes seized arms, provisions,

---

92. Journals of the House of Burgesses, 1702-1712,
270, 276, 282, 284, 288, 292, 298; Hening, Statutes, III,
537-538.

93. Journals of the House of Burgesses, 1712-1716,
p. 360.

94. Ibid., 1712-1726, p. 395.

95. Executive Journals of Colonial Virginia, IV,
462-463.

and tools and made off for the mountains. The search
party found them already settled in a secluded area,
where they had even begun to clear ground for crops. A
brief exchange of gunfire brought about the surrender
cf the slaves, however, and their small colony was destroyed.[96]

There was more trouble the next year, touched
off by a rumor that former Governor Spotswood, just back
from England, had brought an order from the Crown to free
all Christian slaves. This was more a matter of general
unrest than a concerted plot. The governor, at the time
Gooch, reported that by "keeping the Militia to their
Duty, by Imprisonment and severe whipping of the most
Suspected, this Disturbance was very soon Quashed, and
until about six weeks afterwards we were easy..."[97]
Then there was more trouble. About two hundred slaves
in Norfolk and Princess Anne counties gathered on a

---

96. Virginia Magazine, XXVIII (October, 1920),
299-300.

97. Ibid., XXXII (October, 1924), 322-323. Also,
see above, p. 124 for the relation between this unrest
and Anglican missionary efforts among the Virginia Negroes.

Sunday at church time and elected officers to lead an intended rebellion. In this instance four of the Negroes involved were executed.[98] A certain amount of continuing uneasiness is reflected in Gooch's address to the Assembly in 1736, in which he recommended strengthening the militia as a means of policing the slaves; in his proclamation of October 29, 1736, on the same subject; and in the 1738 revision of the law requesting the militia to include a system of four-men patrols to police slave quarters and suspected gathering places of Negroes in every county.[99]

Another unsettled period occurred in and near Williamsburg during the 1770's. The number of runaways advertised seemed noticeably large, and accounts of trouble with slaves in York, James City, and Hanover counties circulated in newspapers as far away as New York.[100] This was in part responsible for the

---

98. Virginia Magazine, XXXII (October, 1924), 322-323.

99. Journals of the House of Burgesses, 1727-1740, p. 243; Executive Journals of Colonial Virginia, IV, 383, 470-471; Hening, Statutes, V, 19, 24.

100. Maryland Gazette, February 8, 1770; New York Journal or General Advertiser, February 15, 1770.

establishment of a night watch in Williamsburg in 1772
to consist of four people to patrol the streets, cry the
hours, and "use their best Endeavours to preserve Peace
and good Order, by apprehending and bringing to Justice
all disorderly People, Slaves, as well as others."[101]
About the same time there was a strict patrol in Yorktown, and Negroes found on the street were picked up and
held overnight.[102]

For supression of an incipient revolt the colony relied largely on the county militia and, after 1738,
the system of Patrols, reinforced by such local activity
as the Williamsburg night watch. From what we know about
the colonial militia, it is not likely that these men
were over-diligent, until there was an indication of
trouble. Still, the colony proved able to act swiftly
in an emergency. Real emergencies, however, were relatively infrequent; for well-laid plots by slaves were
much rarer in eighteenth-century Virginia than what could
be more correctly described as periods of unusual res-
tiveness.

---

101. Virginia Gazette (Purdie and Dixon), July 16, 1772.

102. Ibid., (Pinkney), August 10, 1775.

Chapter XI

THE IMPACT OF THE REVOLUTION

        Until the American Revolution deepened into a
struggle expressed partly in terms of establishing human
liberty, it occurred to few Virginians--or for that matter to few of the colonists anywhere--to question the
existence of chattel slavery on moral grounds. The long
attempt to discourage new importations of Negroes, once
regarded as based on such objections, has been found to
have its real roots in social and economic considerations
and to stress control, not prohibition of the slave trade.
The humanitarian effort to Christianize and educate the
Negro obviously rested upon a moral awareness of sorts,
but it viewed slavery as either actually or potentially
a civilizing institution and therefore productive of good.
        Undoubtedly a relatively large number of people
sensed a certain evil about slavery. Their favorite line
of reasoning was that it degraded master and bondsman a-
like. If anything, they asserted, the owner paid the

greater price, because he was encouraged in idleness and profligacy by his human wealth.[1] This was a sentiment which arose more out of a sense of frustration than a desire for action. Indeed most of its adherents would have condemned any wholesale attack on slavery as a hopeless complication of an already touchy problem. Moreover, few of these people really believed the Negro possessed the degree of humanity requisite for life in a free society.

New arrivals in the colony, having had no chance to accustom themselves gradually to the idea of living in daily contact with slavery, sometimes were in for a shock. Robert Beverley, soon after reaching Virginia, wrote to Edward Athawes that he felt "an Aversion to Slavery; 'tis something so very contradictory to Humanity, that I am really ashamed of my Country whenever I consider of it; & if ever I bid adieu to Virginia, it will be from that Cause alone..."[2] Something of the same sense of revulsion is apparent in Governor Fauquier's will:

---

1. Virginia Gazette, April 10, 1752.

2. Robert Beverley to Edward Athawes, July 11, 1761, in Robert Beverley Letterbook, Manuscript Division, Library of Congress.

It is now expedient that I should dispose
of my slaves, a part of my estate in its
nature disagreeable to me, but which my situation made necessary for me; the disposal of
which has constantly given me uneasiness whenever the thought occured to me. I hope I shall
be found to have been a merciful Master to them
and that no one of them will rise up in judge-
ment against me in that Great Day when all my
actions will be exposed to Public view., For
with what face can I expect mercy from an
offended God, if I have not myself shewn mercy
to these dependant on me. But it is not sufficient that I have been this Master in my life,
I must provide for them at my death, by using
my utmost endeavors that they experience as
little misery during their lives as their very
unhappy and pitiable condition will allow.[3]

Fauquier then went on to stipulate that the slaves in his

estate be allowed to choose their new masters within six

months and that a new owner so designated should have the

right to purchase them at a quarter below the market price.

Children were also not to be separated from their mothers.

Those who were not purchased under these conditions could

then be purchased by the executors and after that sold in

the regular way. The extant records of the executors do

not make it clear to what extent the governor's wishes

were followed, but the slaves were sold here in Williamsburg.

---

3. York County Records, Wills and Inventories, Book
21, pp. 397-403.

Concrete proposals that slavery in the colony
be abolished were rare, ineffective, and certainly unrep-
resentative of the prevailing climate of opinion. There
was a curious letter signed with the pseudonym, Philo-
Bombastia, which appeared in the Virginia Gazette in
1752 and advocated full religious toleration, the ad-
mission of all foreigners, and the freeing of the Negroes in order to make Virginia a land of liberty and
moderation rivalling Pennsylvania.[4] About the only organized anti-slavery movement in Virginia before independence was that of the small Quaker remnant. One of
its leaders, Robert Pleasants of Henrico County corre-
sponded widely with anti-slavery men elsewhere, made
some efforts to influence the General Assembly against
slavery in the 1770's and seems to have attempted individual acts of manumission in violation of the existing
laws.[5] The Cedar Creek Meeting in Hanover County

---

4. Virginia Gazette, March 20, 1752.

5. Adair P. Archer, "The Quaker's Attitude Towards
the Revolution," William and Mary Quarterly, 2nd ser.,
I, (July, 1921), 168; "Letters of Robert Pleasants of
Curles," ibid., 2nd ser., I (April, 1921), 109; 2nd ser.,
II (October, 1922), 274-275.

became another center of Quaker resistance to slavery.[6]

It was difficult to conceive of outright abolition, however, when even a private act of manumission continued to be nearly impossible. The 1691 law prohibiting the freeing of a Negro unless voted by the Assembly in recognition of some meritorious deed or unless the slave were transported out of the colony by his owner continued in effect, reinforced by a similar act in 1723.[7] From time to time the Assembly used its power to free a slave by law, but always sparingly.[8] From the will of Philip Ludwell, dated February 28, 1767, it would also seem that an occasional owner met the burdensome demand of taking a slave from the colony in order to manumit him.[9] Ludwell provided that two girls, Jane and Sarah, should be carried to England and there set

---

6. Mrs. Douglas Summers Brown, "Cedar Creek Monthly Meeting and Its Meeting House," William and Mary Quarterly, 2nd ser., XIX (July, 1939), 293.

7. William Waller Hening, (ed.), The Statutes at Large Being a Collection of all the Laws of Virginia (Richmond, Va., etc., 1810-1823), III, 87-88; IV, 132.

8. Ibid., III, 537-538.

9. Virginia Magazine of History and Biography, XXXII (July, 1924), 288.

free in order to fulfill a promise to Cress, the mother
of the girls, who had been a faithful nurse to Ludwell's
own children.

The years of political controversy with Great
Britain which preceded the outbreak of actual war had the
net effect, so far as the position of the Negro was concerned, of reopening the old question of importing new
blacks. It became possible now to oppose the trade as
one more part of the economic weapon of non-importation.
Thus the 1769 Association contained an article pledging
those who signed not to buy Negroes who had not been on
the continent at least a year.[10] The Burgesses in the
spring of 1771 unsuccessfully addressed the governor
with a request that he approve legislation which would
close the slave trade.[11] The Virginia Convention which
met in the fall of 1774 agreed not to allow the overseas
slave trade to continue.[12] Although some of the protests

---

10. Journals of the House of Burgesses, 1766-1769,
xli.

11. Ibid., 1770-1772, pp. 283-284.

12. Virginia Gazette (Purdie and Dixon), August 11,
1774.

were stated to rest on a desire to end "a Wicked, Cruel
& unnatural Trade," the motivation of the colonial leaders was much more the same blend of fear of civil dis-
order and of damaging the economy that had now prevailed
for virtually a whole century.[13]

The wave of shocked disbelief and bitter anger
that greeted Lord Dunmore's offer in 1775 to free slaves
who joined him is proof enough that the leaders of the
Virginia Patriots had not yet brought themselves to the
point of considering emancipation. The circumstances of
the governor's move, which did more than anything else
to render him hateful in the eyes of the colony, are familiar. Claiming to have been driven from Williamsburg
as an aftermath of the removal of the powder from the
Public Magazine in April, 1775, Dunmore had moved by
stages to the harbor of Norfolk, where under the protection of his ships, he was maintaining a shadowy government.

Finally, one of his desperation moves was a
proclamation of November 7, 1775, offering among other
things to free any servants or Negro slaves who would

---

13. Virginia Magazine, XVIII (April, 1910), 166-167.

come in to his side and bear arms against the rebellious
colonists.[14] The combination of arms and freedom for
slaves sent a sickening fear through the Virginians, who
saw in Dunmore's "Damned, infernal, Diabolical proclamation" not so much the potential defeat of their own political effort as the undermining of society itself.[15]

Although there were a number of derisive comments, such as the account in Purdie's Gazette of the
formidable, eighty-man "Royal Regiment of Black Fusiliers"
marching to the martial tune of "Hungry Niger, parch'd
Corn!" Virginians were inclined, if anything to become
unreasonable in their fear.[16] However, Dunmore's move
was one of desperation, and the danger was not really so
great. The militia organization was then about as effective as it would be during the entire war, and events had

14. Francis L. Berkeley, Jr., Dunmore's Proclamation
of Emancipation (Charlottesville, Va., 1941), frontispiece;
Benjamin Quarles, "Lord Dunmore As Liberator," William and
and Mary Quarterly, 3rd ser., XV (October, 1958), 494-507.

15. John Hatley Norton to John Norton, [October 16,
1775?] in Francis Hatley Norton, (ed.), John Norton & Sons
Merchants of London and Virginia (Richmond, Va., 1937),
pp. 391-392; Virginia Magazine, XIV (January, 1907), 253.

16. Virginia Gazette (Purdie), March 22, 1776.

already been set in motion which led to the decisive defeat the Loyalists suffered at Great Bridge the following
month. The Virginia Convention hastened to provide the
death penalty for slaves recaptured from Dunmore, though
it offered to pardon those who left him voluntarily, and
various writers to the Virginia Gazette began to counter
Dunmore's appeal.[17]

Still, Dunmore's offer of freedom filtered
through to slaves in a great many places, and a certain
number of them tried to reach the British base at Norfolk.[18]
Some were already there who had escaped before the formal
proclamation, been seized by British raiding parties, or
been brought in by Loyalist masters.[19] Rumors around
Williamsburg placed the number of former slaves with
Dunmore as high as two thousand, but the Negro troops

---

17. The Proceedings of the Convention of Delegates
Held at the Town of Richmond...on Friday, the 1st of December, 1775 (Richmond, Va., 1816), p. 66; Virginia Gazette
(Purdie), November 17, 1765; (Dixon and Hunter), November 25, December 16, 1775.

18. Virginia Gazette (Purdie), January 26, 1776.

19. David J. Mays, Edmund Pendleton, 1721-1803: A
Biography (Cambridge, Mass., 1952), II, 56; Virginia
Gazette (Dixon and Hunter), October 28, 1775; Virginia
Magazine, XVII (April, 1909), 167-168.

actually under arms at the Battle of Great Bridge numbered about three or four hundred. In all, some eight hundred Negroes perhaps reached Dunmore.[20]

Dunmore's defeat at Great Bridge and the subsequent evacuation of Norfolk reduced him more to the status of a nuisance than a real menace, although he was to continue to harass the coast for several months. His ships carried a number of the Negroes along, and all through the spring of 1776 there continued to be slaves who slipped off, sometimes in a stolen boat or canoe, to join Dunmore.[21] In a number of cases they were intercepted by the Patriots and returned to their owners, sold at auction, or occasionally executed.[22] A worse fate awaited many of those who actually reached the British; for both on their ships and at Dunmore's last

---

20. Virginia Gazette (Dixon and Hunter), December 2, 1775; Quarles, "Lord Dunmore as Liberator," p. 506.

21. Virginia Gazette (Dixon and Hunter), February 3, 1776.

22. Ibid., (Purdie), March 29, 1776; (Dixon and Hunter), April 13, 1776.

headquarters on Gwynn's Island fever and smallpox took

a horrible toll.[23]

For that matter the unrest promoted by the war

kept the Negro population stirred up all through the next

several years. Whenever the British were operating in

Virginia, there were always a certain number of Negroes

who escaped to the enemy or were captured on coastal

raids.[24] Others simply ran off into hiding; the figures

for fugitives remained unusually high throughout the Rev-

olution. Jefferson estimated 30,000 in the one year of

1778.[25]

There were also Negro troops fighting on the

Patriot side, perhaps about five thousand during the

course of the war. Largely at Washington's insistence,

Negroes were at first excluded from Continental enlist-

ments by orders of July 9 and November 12, 1775. Concern

---

23. Virginia Gazette (Purdie), March 8, 1776; (Dixon
and Hunter), June 15, July 20, 1776.

24. Ibid., (Purdie), September 19, November 28,
1777; "Diary of Landon Carter," William and Mary Quarterly,
1st ser., XX (January, 1912), 176, 178-179, 182-183, 185.

25. John Hope Franklin, From Slavery to Freedom: A
History of American Negroes (New York, 1948), p. 133.

about the effect of Dunmore's Proclamation, however,
quickly persuaded the American commander to change his
mind; and from December 1, 1775, free Negroes were accepted in the Continental Army.[26] The majority of Negro
troops thereafter enlisted came from the Northern colonies, and, with the exception of two special companies
from Rhode Island and Connecticut, they were scattered
through existing regiments.[27]

A small number of Virginia Negroes, slaves as
well as freemen, saw active military and naval service.
In 1776, free mulattoes were permitted to serve as drum-
mers, pipers, and pioneers, these being duties not normally requiring the bearing of arms.[28] A rumor that
slaves could win freedom by fighting was also circulating, to such an extent that a 1777 law required recruit-
ing officers to see that any Negro they enlisted could
provide a certificate of freedom.[29] This law implies

---

26. Franklin, Slavery to Freedom, pp. 131-133. The
most recent full-scale treatment of the Negro in the Revolution is Benjamin Quarles, The Negro in the American
Revolution (Chapel Hill, 1961).

27. Franklin, Slavery to Freedom, pp. 134-137.

28. Ibid., p. 134.

29. Hening, Statutes, IX, 280.

that free Negroes by then were being accepted for full
military service.

A certain amount of illegal enlistment of
slaves continued to go on throughout the war, in some
cases because the rumor still persisted that freedom
could be won and in others because slaveowners fraudu-
lently represented them as freemen and then used them as
substitutes for free white men.[30] Then, at the conclusion of the war, the owner expected to reclaim a Negro
substitute as a slave.[31] The sordid character of this
procedure influenced the legislature to vote in 1783 to
free slaves who had been enlisted in this way.[32] A few
special acts conferring freedom on slaves for meritorious
service during the war were also passed in the 1780's.
One of the more notable examples was James Armistead,
who had been of conspicuous assistance to Lafayette.[33]

---

30. Virginia Gazette (Purdie), April 11, 1777.

31. The Negro in Virginia. Compiled by the Writers'
Program of the Work Projects Administration (New York,
1940), pp. 23-24.

32. Hening, Statutes, XI, 308-309.

33. Ibid., X, 115, 211, 372; XII, 380-381; XIII,
102, 103, 618-620.

Many slaves in Virginia were already experienced boatmen and pilots long before the war with Great Britain had begun. A number of them were used to fill out the crews of Virginia naval vessels and in one case to command a vessel.[34]

The real importance of the American Revolution to the Negro was not, however, the limited opportunity it gave him to participate as a soldier. Rather it was the fact that large numbers of Americans for the first time began to grasp the inconsistency of slavery and the doctrines of natural rights on which they had based their own struggle for political independence. How far the correction of this inconsistency progressed depended very closely upon geography. In the Northern colonies the tide of revolutionary spirit swept away the very institution of slavery, and as far south as Virginia and North Carolina serious inroads were made before a reaction set in.[35]

---

34. Negro in Virginia, p. 21; Virginia Historical Register, I, 80, 129, 131.

35. Ulrich B. Phillips, American Negro Slavery (New York, 1918), pp. 115-121; J. R. Brackett, "Status of Slave, 1775-1789," Essays in Constitutional History. Edited by J. Franklin Jameson. (Boston and New York, 1889).

Some of the individual leaders of the revolutionary movement in the colony, being more at home with theories of liberty and more aware of the demands of logic, began to nibble at the edges of the problem before 1776. In his celebrated defense of a mulatto indentured servant before the General Court in 1770, Jefferson had pleaded the universality of human freedom without qualification in an effort to end the man's obligated service.[36] Jefferson also recalled joining Richard Bland about this time in trying to win a moderate extension of legal protection to slaves.[37] Both these efforts came to nothing. Patrick Henry was on record in 1773 that slavery was "repugnant to humanity," though he admitted that he was a slaveholder himself, "drawn along by the general inconvenience of living without them."[38]

---

36. Dumas Malone, Jefferson the Virginian (Boston, 1948), pp. 121-122.

37. James E. Pate, "Richard Bland's Inquiry Into the Rights of the British Colonies," William and Mary Quarterly, 2nd ser., XI, No. 1 (January, 1931), 20.

38. James Curtis Ballagh, A History of Slavery in Virginia (Baltimore, 1902), p. 130.

The work of the Virginia Convention of 1776
served to draw the lines between those who believed the
implications of the American struggle for independence
had to be carried out to the extent of abolishing slavery
and those more cautious men who were troubled on this
score neither by logic or liberality. In the first article of the Declaration of Rights, with its unqualified
assertion that "all men are by nature equally free," the
issue was joined most clearly; so it is not surprising
that there was debate on the relevance of this very point
to slavery. Robert Carter Nicholas, and perhaps others,
attacked the first article as an invitation to "civil
convulsion." The anti-slavery men certainly did not re-
veal their hands at this time, however, for they answered,
"not without inconsistency" as Edmund Randolph observed,
that slaves were not "constituent members" of society and
could derive no benefit from the Virginia Declaration of
Rights.[39]

There is no avoiding the fact that this refusal
to admit the Negro might benefit from the Virginia

---

39. "Edmund Randolph's Essay on the Revolutionary
History of Virginia," Virginia Magazine of History and
Biography, XLIV (January, 1936), 45.

Declaration of Rights was the majority view. It was not, however, the view of Mason, the author of that first article, nor of Jefferson or George Wythe and of others who had kept silent during the debate. Nor was discussion of the relevance of slavery to the Revolution yet over. Jefferson and Wythe were named to the committee created that same summer to make a systematic revision of the laws of the Commonwealth, and one of the tasks the two men set for themselves was to write a plan of emancipation into law.[40] And the issue continued to be debated elsewhere--in the meetings of Phi Beta Kappa and in the columns of the Gazette, where an opponent of slavery reminded an adversary

> ...to read with attention the first section
> of the declaration of rights, and to place
> his slaves in the situation so justly de-
> clared to be the natural right of all man-
> kind, for 'till that be done the talk of
> justice is far from being completed...[41]

The impact of the American Revolution on the institution of slavery in Virginia by no means expended

---

40. Phillips, American Negro Slavery, p. 122; Thomas Jefferson, Notes on Virginia. Edited by William Peden (Chapel Hill, N. C., 1955), p. 137.

41. William and Mary Quarterly, 1st ser., IV, 225; Virginia Gazette (Dixon and Nicolson), April 1, 1780.

itself in the years between 1776 and 1783. It was a continuing movement which had some degree of vitality over the last two decades of the eighteenth century. Among those who sought to alleviate the position of Negroes within the new state three separate objectives became apparent: the prohibition of the overseas slave trade, the legalizing of private manumission, and the emancipation of slaves by public law. One of these was a complete success, one achieved momentary fulfillment, and the third ended in absolute failure.

The importation of slaves from Africa had been in abeyance for two years before independence and under attack for much longer. Consequently, its permanent repeal by the legislature in 1778 caused no difficulty.[42] The new statute, in fact, applied not only to the overseas trade but to Negroes brought into Virginia by land as well, although there was a loophole to protect bona fide masters moving into the state with their Negroes. Slaves introduced into the state in violation of this law were entitled to freedom, and eventually, in 1795, the

---

42. Hening, Statutes, IX, 471-472.

procedure by which a slave might bring suit for freedom
under this law became relatively simple.[43]

Initially, sentiment was running fairly
strongly in favor of permitting any master who cared to
do so to free his slaves, even though this had been contrary to colonial practice. In a number of cases owners
began to leave wills instructing that certain slaves be
freed, though the law had not yet been altered to allow
this.[44] But in the case of John Barr of Northumberland
County the Assembly proceeded to recognize such an act
of manumission in 1777.[45] In other instances the Assembly
voted a number of years later to legalize such wills.[46]

The rewriting of the law to permit voluntary
manumission without the danger of complications like
these occurred in 1782.[47] Slaves so liberated were free
to continue to reside within the state, the only real

---

43. Hening, Statutes, X, 307-308; XII, 182-183;
Ballagh, Slavery in Virginia, pp. 123-124.

44. Ballagh, Slavery in Virginia, p. 120.

45. Hening, Statutes, IX, 320-321.

46. Ibid., XII, 611-616.

47. Ibid., XI, 39-40.

restriction being one which was placed on the former

master, namely, to be financially responsible for freed

Negroes who were too old or too young to support them-

selves. County records of the 1780's and 1790's contain

numerous examples of wills in which masters took advan-

tage of the new law.[48] Some obviously rewarded only a

particularly faithful servant or two, others outlined

comprehensive schemes which were designed to free all of

their Negroes in stages over a period of years. Many

heaped recriminations upon themselves and their fellows

for having acted "in contradition of their own delcara-

tion of Rights, and in violation of every sacred law of

Nature." There are estimates which place the average

number of manumissions at a thousand per year during the

first decade in which the law was in force.[49]

The idealism and moral fervor which had pro-

duced this wave of voluntary manumissions was doomed to

---

48. For example, see York County Records, Wills and
Inventories, Book 23, p. 685; Hening, Statutes, XI, 362-
363; Virginia Magazine, II (October, 1894), 210; XX (January,1912), 110; XXIV (January, 1916), 73-74; LVI (July,
1948), 348-349; William and Mary Quarterly, 1st ser.,
IX (July, 1900), 27n; XI (October, 1902), 139.

49. Ballagh, Slavery in Virginia, p. 121.

be short-lived; for there soon began to be a sharp reaction from owners who declined to free their own slaves
and who found the new freemen a disruptive element in
their localities. The experience of Robert Carter of
Nomini Hall is a good example of what happened. Carter,
whose motivation in so doing was primarily religious,
but also partly economic, worked out in 1791 a scheme
for gradually freeing his slaves, an undertaking rendered
the more spectacular by the fact that he was one of the
largest slaveholders in the colony with Negroes scattered
out over many different landholdings. He proposed to begin by setting free thirty older slaves in 1791 with an
additional number gaining their freedom every January 2
through the year 1812.[50] The flood of protests mounted
steadily from planters living near lands on which some
of the Negroes had been manumitted. One letter which came
in anonymously from Frederick County complained that:

> ...a man has almost as good a right to set
> fire to his own building though his neigh-
> bors is to be destroyed by it, as to free
> his slaves...[51]

---

50. Louis Morton, Robert Carter of Nomini Hall
(Williamsburg, Va., 1941), pp. 251-265.

51. Ibid., p. 266.

Eventually the whole scheme broke down with Carter's death. His sons were not anxious to see it completed and probably only a small number of the Negroes ever really benefitted.[52] Finally, protests similar to those which had poured in upon Robert Carter caused a revision of the 1782 law in 1805 that went back to colonial precedents and allowed owners to free slaves only if the Negroes then left the state.[53] With this action the Revolution became a dead letter, so far as slavery in Virginia was concerned.

The third and most sweeping objective, the emancipation of Virginia's slaves, was never more than a straw in the wind. The motivation for seeking this arose not from the political principles of the Revolution alone but also from religious conviction, notably among the Quakers and some Baptists, and from more hard-headed economic reasoning that tobacco was bound to decline and render slave labor unprofitable. Singly or collectively, these remained, however, distinctly minority views.

---

52. Morton, Robert Carter of Nomini Hall, pp. 268-269.

53. Helen T. Catterall, (ed.), Judicial Cases Concerning American Slavery and the Negro (Washington, 1924-1926), I, 73-74.

In their work on the committee to revise the
laws of the state Wythe and Jefferson evolved a plan
for emancipation which they planned to introduce in the
legislature of 1779. Briefly, they would have freed
slaves born after the passage of the act, provided for
their education in "tillage, arts or sciences," and then
have arranged for their settlement outside the state.
As it turned out, the two men did not even attempt to
get consideration of their proposal.[54]

There were also some organized efforts from
the Quakers, primarily petitions to the legislature.
Before the voluntary manumission law of 1782, these had
been appeals for recognition of the right of the Quakers
to free their own Negroes. Subsequently there was at
least one petition for general emancipation, during the
session of 1785, but it was rejected by unanimous vote.[55]

Although a few men continued to hope, as
Washington did, that slavery might "be abolished by slow,
sure and imperceptible degrees," there was in reality only

---

54. Jefferson, Notes on Virginia, p. 137.

55. Brackett, "Status of Slave," pp. 303-307.

one other noteworthy effort to revive emancipation.[56]
This was the appearance of St. George Tucker's <u>Disserta-
tion on Slavery with a Proposal for the Gradual Abolition
of It in the State of Virginia</u>, published and presented
to the legislature in 1796, where it was promptly dis-
missed from consideration. Tucker reprinted it as an
appendix to his edition of Blackstone in 1803, but emancipation as a political issue did not really come alive
again until the great debates of 1831-1832.[57]

Both the writings of Jefferson and Tucker,
who had more to say about ending slavery than any other
Virginians of this era, make it clear that even the minority who would have freed the slaves based their proposals on the assumption that emancipation had to be
carried out gradually and that it had to include colonization. It was also obvious that they, no less than the

---

56. Phillips, <u>American Negro Slavery</u>, p. 123.

57. Tucker's pamphlet is most readily available
in Mrs. George P. Coleman, (ed.), <u>Virginia Silhouettes</u>:
<u>Contemporary Letters Concerning Negro Slavery in the
State of Virginia</u> (Richmond, Va., 1934), Appendix.

defenders of slavery, regarded the Negro as an inferior
being, incapable of assimilation into free society in
Virginia.[58]

So far then as slavery and the Negro were concerned, the American Revolution offered in Virginia a few
years of hope and little more. The end of the overseas
trade in 1778 and the recognition of voluntary manumission
in 1782 marked a considerable beginning, but slavery
proved to be a problem of such deep social and economic
consequences as not to be susceptible to gradual solutions.
In a few years Virginia's profitable export of Negroes in
the domestic trade would replace the overseas commerce in
human flesh. The right of an individual to free his own
slaves was once again sharply restricted. And the emancipation movement, weak enough in any event, would be
displaced by a colonization movement, doomed by its spirit
of condescension and its impracticality.

---

58. Tucker, Dissertation on Slavery, p. 51ff;
Jefferson, Notes on Virginia, p. 138ff. Tucker simply
quotes at length from Jefferson on this point, but this
certainly indicates that both men agreed on the Negro's
inferiority.

Chapter XII

THE NEGRO'S ROLE IN COLONIAL WILLIAMSBURG: A SUMMARY

When all the evidence is in concerning the Negro population of eighteenth-century Williamsburg--and it is unfortunately little enough information--perhaps what remains as the most important single feature of the Negro's life here is the simple fact that slaves were about half the resident population of the capital. Because they were a subjugated, inarticulate, leaderless half it becomes simple enough to forget how much they must have influenced life in Williamsburg and all but impossible to arrive at an adequate estimate of that influence.

Sooner or later every part of the civilization of colonial Virginia bore the impress of slavery. It helped, for instance, to build up the stratified society characteristic of Virginia; and at the same time it partially destroyed the mobility that was also a feature of this society. Some aspects of the life of the colony, such as the organization of society, law, custom, or the place of religion, are areas in which Williamsburg serves conveniently as a specific example of what was largely true in the whole of the Tidewater and Piedmont.

Economically, Williamsburg was neither so important nor so typical. Lacking a share in the slave trade, not inhabited by large numbers of field slaves, and possibly not even well populated with Negro craftsmen, the town utilized its slaves largely as domestics. This was a society, however, in which household labor was important. Furthermore, slave property undoubtedly comprised a significant proportion of Williamsburg's wealth.

It was in the life of the Negro himself that Williamsburg may have been most distinctive. Here the slave seemed to be more fully adjusted to white society, more skilled at domestic tasks, to a degree better educated, and perhaps more restive under the yoke of slavery than on the plantation. There should be sober realism, however, about the hardship of the average slave's life. Even in town, living conditions were almost certainly primitive and regimentation as strict as it could be made.

With consideration of the impact of the American Revolution on slavery, Williamsburg comes back into the mainstream of the development of Virginia, for the political battles fought and the political principles established here belong to the history of the whole colony and state, and indeed to the whole nation. In the matter of slavery, however, it must be admitted that, so far as the Southern colonies were concerned, the spirit of the Revolution was at its least triumphant.

As a last word, we ought perhaps to come back to an extremely simple, unpretentious point, that is, how much the slaves were a part of the ordinary daily life of Williamsburg and how frequently they would have been seen at work, along the street, or perhaps on the fringes of some large public gathering.

BIBLIOGRAPHY

(Note: This is not intended to be a complete bibliography
on the history of the Negro in Virginia. It is
restricted to materials which were particularly
useful in the preparation of this report.)

I Bibliographical Aids

Cappon, Lester J. and Duff, Stella F., (eds.), Virginia
Gazette Index, 1736-1780, 2 vols. Williamsburg,
Va.: Institute of Early American History and Cul-
ture, 1950.

Hampton Institute, A Classified Catalog of the Negro
Collection in the C. P. Huntington Library,
Hampton Institute. Hampton, Va.: Hampton Institute,
1940.

Swem, Earl Gregg, (comp.), Virginia Historical Index,
2 vols. Roanoke, Va.: 1934-1936.

Work, Monroe N., (ed.), Bibliography of the Negro in
Africa and America. New York: 1928.

II Printed Sources

Arber, Edward, (ed.), Travels and Works of Captain John
Smith, 2 vols. Edinburgh: John Grant, 1910.

Bassett, John Spencer, (ed.), The Writings of "Colonel
William Byrd of Westover in Virginia Esqr." New
York: Doubleday, Page & Co. 1901.

Berkeley, Francis L. Jr., Dunmore's Proclamation of Emancipation. Charlottesville, Va.: Tracey W. McGregor Library, University of Virginia, 1941.

Byrd I, William, "Letters of..." Virginia Magazine of History and Biography, XXIV (1916), 225-237, 350-360; XXV (1917), 43-52, 128-138, 250-264, 352-364; XXVI (1918), 17-31, 124-134, 247-259, 388-392; XXVII (1919), 117-168, 273-288; XXVIII (1920), 11-28.

Carter, Col. Landon, "Diary of..." William and Mary Quarterly, 1st series, XIII (1904-1905), 45-53, 157-164, 219-224; XIV (1905-06), 38-44, 181-186, 246-253; XV (1906-07), 15-20, 86-87, 205-211; XVI (1907-08), 149-156, 256-268; XVII (1908-09), 9-18; XVIII (1909-10), 37-44; XX (1911-12), 173-186; XXI (1912-13), 172-181.

Catterall, Helen T., (ed.), Judicial Cases Concerning American Slavery and the Negro, 5 vols. Washington: Carnegie Institution, 1924-1926.

Coleman, Mrs. George P., (ed.), Virginia Silhouettes: Contemporary Letters Concerning Negro Slavery in the State of Virginia. Richmond, Va.: The Dietz Printing Company, 1934.

Donnan, Elizabeth, (ed.), Documents Illustrative of the History of the Slave Trade to America. Volume IV: The Border Colonies and Southern Colonies. Washington: Carnegie Institution, 1935.

Evans, Emory G., (ed.), "A Question of Complexion: Documents Concerning the Negro and the Franchise in Eighteenth-Century Virginia," Virginia Magazine of History and Biography, LXXI (October, 1963), 411-415.

Farish, Hunter Dickinson, (ed.), Journals and Letters of Philip Vickers Fithian, 1773-1774: A Plantation Tutor of the Old Dominion. Williamsburg, Va.: Colonial Williamsburg, Inc., 1943.

Fisher, George [Daniel], "Narrative of..." William and
    Mary Quarterly, 1st series, XVII (1908-1909), 100-
    139, 147-176.

Fitzhugh, William, "Letters of..." Virginia Magazine of
    History and Biography, I (1893-94), 17-55, 105-126,
    253-277, 391-410; II (1894-95), 15-36, 121-142, 259-
    275, 370-379; III (1895-96), 1-15, 161-168, 253-261,
    369-373; IV (1896-97), 67-74, 176-184, 310-312, 415-
    420; V (1897-98), 29-33, 169-173, 297-302; VI (1898-
    99), 60-72, 158-162.

Gordon, Col. James, "Journal of...of Lancaster County,
    Va." William and Mary Quarterly, 1st series, XI
    (1902-1903), 98-112, 217-236; XII (1903-1904), 1-12.

Hening, William Waller, (ed.), The Statutes at Large
    Being a Collection of all the Laws of Virginia, 13
    vols. Richmond, Va., etc.: [Printed for the Editor],
    1810-1823.

Jefferson, Thomas, Notes on Virginia. Edited by William
    Peden. Chapel Hill, N. C.: University of North
    Carolina Press, 1955.

Kingsbury, Susan Myra, (ed.), The Records of the Virginia
    Company of London, 4 vols. Washington: Government
    Printing Office, 1906-1935.

Knight, Edgar W., (ed.), A Documentary History of Educa-
    tion in the South Before 1860, 5 vols. Chapel Hill,
    N. C.: University of North Carolina Press, 1949-1953.

McIlwaine, H. R. and Hall, Wilmer L., (eds.), Executive
    Journals of the Council of Colonial Virginia, 5 vols.
    Richmond, Va.: The Virginia State Library, 1925-1945.

McIlwaine, H. R. and Kennedy, J. P., (eds.), Journals of
    the House of Burgesses of Virginia, 13 vols. Richmond,
    Va.: The Virginia State Library, 1905-1915.

Mason, Frances Norton, (ed.), John Norton & Sons Merchants
    of London and Virginia. Richmond, Va.: The Dietz
    Press, 1937.

Maxwell, William, (ed.), "Smyth's Travels in Virginia, in 1773," Virginia Historical Register, VI (1853), 11-20, 77-90, 131-148.

Perry, William Stevens, (ed.), Historical Collections Relating to the American Colonial Church, Volume I. Hartford, Conn.: Printed for the Subscribers, 1870.

Pleasants, Robert, "Letters of...of Curles," William and Mary Quarterly, 2nd series, I, (April, 1921), 107-113; II (October, 1922), 257-275.

Shelley, Fred, (ed.), "The Journal of Ebenezer Hazard in Virginia, 1777," Virginia Magazine of History and Biography, LXII (October, 1954), 400-423.

Stanard, William G., (ed.), "Some Notes on 'Green Spring,'" Virginia Magazine of History and Biography, XXXVII (1929), 289-300; XXXVIII (1930), 38-50.

United States, First Census of the United States, 1790: Records of the State Enumerations: 1782-1785: Virginia. Washington: Government Printing Office, 1908.

Virginia, The Proceedings of the Convention of Delegates Held at the Town of Richmond...on Friday, the 1st of December, 1775. Richmond, Va.: Ritchie, Truehart & Duval, 1816.

Virginia Historical Society, "Randolph Manuscript," Virginia Magazine of History and Biography, XV (1907-1908), 390-405; XVI (1908), 1-15, 113-131; XVII (1909), 1-13, 113-132, 225-248, 337-351; XVIII (1910), 1-24, 129-139, 241-255, 353-373; XIX (1911), 1-12, 149-156, 240-247, 337-347; XX (1912), 1-13, 113-126, 225-235, 337-346; XXI (1913), 1-8, 113-121, 225-233, 347-358; XXII (1914), 14-21, 113-121, 225-231, 337-347.

Wright, Louis B. and Tinling, Marion, (eds.), The Secret Diary of William Byrd of Westover. Richmond, Va.: The Deitz Press, 1941.

III   Manuscript Sources

Robert Beverley Letterbook, 1761-1791. 1 volume. Manuscripts Division, Library of Congress. (Colonial
Williamsburg microfilm).

Campbell-Preston Papers. Manuscripts Division, Library
of Congress. (Colonial Williamsburg microfilm).

Dawson Papers, 1728-1775. Manuscripts Division, Library
of Congress. (Colonial Williamsburg microfilm).

Fulham Palace Manuscripts, Virginia. British Transcripts,
Library of Congress. (Colonial Williamsburg microfilm).

William Hugh Grove Diary, University of Virginia. (Colonial Williamsburg photostat).

Journal of Meetings of President and Masters, College of
William and Mary.

Manuscripts of Dr. Bray's Associates, Archives of the
Society for the Propagation of the Gospel in Foreign
Parts. (Colonial Williamsburg microfilm).

Steuart Papers. Historical Society of Pennsylvania.
(Colonial Williamsburg microfilm).

City of Williamsburg, Personal Property Taxes, 1781-1861.
Virginia State Library. (Colonial Williamsburg microfilm).

York County Records. (Colonial Williamsburg microfilm).

IV   Newspapers

Georgia Gazette

Maryland Gazette

New York Journal or General Advertiser

Virginia Gazette

V Secondary Materials

Ames, Susie M., *Studies of the Virginia Eastern Shore in the Seventeenth Century*. Richmond, Va. The Dietz Press, 1940.

Archer, Adair P., "The Quaker's Attitude Towards the Revolution," *William and Mary Quarterly*, 2nd series, I (July, 1921), 167-182.

Ballagh, James Curtis, *A History of Slavery in Virginia*. Baltimore, Md.: Johns Hopkins Press, 1902.

Brackett, J. R., "Status of Slave, 1775-1789," *Essays in Constitutional History*. Edited by J. Franklin Jameson. Boston and New York: Houghton, Mifflin and Co., 1889.

Brown, Mrs. Douglas Summers, "Cedar Creek Monthly Meeting and Its Meeting House," *William and Mary Quarterly*, 2nd series, XIX (July, 1939), 293-298.

Bruce, Philip Alexander, *Economic History of Virginia in the Seventeenth Century*, 2 volumes. New York: Macmillan, 1895-1907.

Craven, Wesley Frank, *The Southern Colonies in the Seventeenth Century*. Baton Rouge, La.: Louisiana State University Press, 1949.

Dalzell, George W., *Benefit of Clergy in America & Related Matters*. Winston-Salem, N. C.: John F. Blair, 1955.

Degler, Carl N., *Out of the Past: The Forces that Shaped Modern America*. New York: Harper & Brothers, 1959.

Degler, Carl N., "Slavery and the Genesis of American Race Prejudice," *Comparative Studies in Society and History*, II (October, 1959), 49-66.

Earnest, Joseph B., *The Religious Development of the Negro in Virginia*. Charlottesville, Va.: The Michie Co., 1914.

Franklin, John Hope, From Slavery to Freedom: A History
     of American Negroes. New York: Alfred A. Knopf,
     1948.

Frazier, E. Franklin, The Negro in the United States.
     New York: Macmillan Co., 1949.

Gewehr, Wesley M., The Great Awakening in Virginia.
     Durham, N. C.: Duke University Press, 1930.

Gipson, Lawrence Henry, The British Empire Before the
     American Revolution, 8 volumes. Caldwell, Idaho
     and New York: Caxton Printers and Alfred A. Knopf,
     1936- .

Goodwin, Mary F., "Christianizing and Educating the Negro
     in Colonial Virginia," Historical Magazine of the
     Protestant Episcopal Church, I (September, 1932),
     143-152.

Goodwin, W. A. R., Historical Sketch of Bruton Church.
     Petersburg, Va.: Franklin Press Co., 1903.

Goodwin, W. A. R., The Record of Bruton Parish Church.
     Edited with revisions and additions by Mary Frances
     Goodwin. Richmond, Va.: The Dietz Press, 1941.

Gray, Lewis Cecil, History of Agriculture in the Southern
     United States to 1860, 2 volumes. New York: Peter
     Smith, 1941.

Greene, Evarts B., and Harrington, Virginia D., American
     Population Before the Federal Census of 1790. New
     York: Columbia University Press, 1932.

Handlin, Oscar and Mary F., "Origins of the Southern
     Labor System," William and Mary Quarterly, 3rd series,
     VII (April, 1950), 199-222.

Jackson, Luther P., "Religious Development of the Negro
     in Virginia from 1760 to 1860," Journal of Negro
     History, XVI (April, 1931), 168-239.

Jackson, Luther P., "Virginia Negro Soldiers and Seamen in the American Revolution," Journal of Negro History, XXVII (July, 1942), 247-287.

Jernegan, Marcus W., Laboring and Dependent Classes in Colonial America, 1607-1783. Chicago: University of Chicago Press, 1931.

Jernegan, Marcus W., "Slavery and Conversion in the American Colonies," American Historical Review, XXI (April, 1916), 504-527.

Jordan, Winthrop D., "Modern Tensions and the Origins of American Slavery," Journal of Southern History, XXVIII (February, 1962), 18-30.

Landrum, Grace W., "The First Colonial Grammar in English," William and Mary Quarterly, 2nd series, XIX (July, 1939), 272-285.

Main, Jackson T., "The One Hundred," William and Mary Quarterly, 3rd series, XI (July, 1954), 354-384.

Malone, Dumas, Jefferson the Virginian. Boston: Little, Brown, 1948.

Marshall, R. W., "What Jonathan Boucher Preached," Virginia Magazine of History and Biography, XLVI (January, 1938), 1-12.

Mays, David J., Edmund Pendleton, 1721-1803: A Biography, 2 vols. Cambridge, Mass.: Harvard University Press, 1952.

Miller, Perry, "The Religious Impulse in the Founding of Virginia: Religion and Society in the Early Literature," William and Mary Quarterly, 3rd series, V (October, 1948), 492-522; VI (January, 1949), 24-41.

Morton, Louis, Robert Carter of Nomini Hall. Williamsburg, Va.: Colonial Williamsburg, Inc., 1941.

Pate, James E., "Richard Bland's Inquiry Into the Rights of the British Colonies," William and Mary Quarterly, 2nd series, XI (January, 1931), 20-28.

Pennington, Edgar L., "Thomas Bray's Associates' Work Among Negroes," American Antiquarian Society Proceedings, new series, XLVIII (1938), 311-403.

Phillips, Ulrich B., American Negro Slavery. New York: Appleton, 1918.

Pinchbeck, Raymond B., "The Virginia Negro Artisan and Tradesman," (Publications of the University of Virginia Phelps-Stokes Fellowship Papers, No. VII) Richmond, Va.: William Byrd Press, 1926.

Quarles, Benjamin, "Lord Dunmore As Liberator," William and Mary Quarterly, 3rd series, XV (October, 1958), 494-507.

Quarles, Benjamin, The Negro in the American Revolution. Chapel Hill, N.C.: The University of North Carolina Press, 1961.

Randolph, Edmund, "...Essay on the Revolutionary History of Virginia," Virginia Magazine of History and Biography, XLIII (1935), 115-138, 209-232, 294-315; XLIV (1936), 35-50, 105-115, 223-231, 312-322; XLV (1937), 46-47.

Read, Allen W., "The Speech of Negroes in Colonial America," Journal of Negro History, XXIV (July, 1939), 247-258.

Russell, John Henderson, The Free Negro in Virginia, 1619-1865. Baltimore, Md.: Johns Hopkins Press, 1913.

Scott, Arthur P., Criminal Law in Colonial Virginia. Chicago: University of Chicago Press, 1930.

Sellers, Leila, Charleston Business on the Eve of the American Revolution. Chapel Hill, N. C.: The University of North Carolina Press, 1934.

Semple, Robert B., _A History of the Rise and Progress of the Baptists in Virginia_. Revised and extended by G. W. Beale. Richmond, Va.: Pitt and Dickinson, 1894.

Stampp, Kenneth M., _The Peculiar Institution: Slavery in the Anti-Bellum South_. New York: Alfred A. Knopf, 1956.

Thompson, H. P., _Thomas Bray_. London: S.P.C.K., 1954.

Trevelyan, George Macaulay, _English Social History_. London, etc.: Longmans, Green and Company, 1947.

U. S. Bureau of the Census, _Historical Statistics of the United States: Colonial Times to 1957_. Washington, U. S. Government Printing Office, 1960.

WPA Virginia (comp.) _The Negro in Virginia_. Compiled by the Writers' Program of the Work Projects Administration. New York: Hastings House, 1940.

VI Reports

Baker, Eliza, "Memoirs of Williamsburg, Virginia," Typescript of conversations between Eliza Baker, an ex-slave, and W. A. R. Goodwin, May 4, 1933, in Colonial Williamsburg Archives.

Goodwin, Mary R. M., (ed.), "William and Mary College Historical Notes," Manuscript Report, Colonial Williamsburg, Inc.

Stephenson, Mary A., (comp.), "Notes on the Negro School in Williamsburg, 1760-1774," Manuscript Report, Colonial Williamsburg, Inc.

INDEX

Shield, James, 132
Smallpox, 219
Society for the Propagation of the Gospel, 119-120
Southall, James, 53, 63
Spotswood, Alexander, Gov., 112, 206
Stafford, Robert, 115
Surry County, 202-205

Taliaferro, Charles, 53
Tamar, Edmund, 196
Tan works, 71
Thompson, Samuel, 204
Thruston, John, 103
Tidewater Negroes, 24, 39
Tithables, Negroes as, 11, 47-49, 121
Trade, slave, domestic, 28-29, 30; imports, 24-33, 88-89,
     91, 209, 214-215, 226-227
Treasurer, ship, 1
Trebell, William, 74, 83, 196
Trials, 165, 168-170
Tucker, St. George, 232-233
Tucker, William, 115
Tuell, Matthew, 54, 68

Valentine, Joseph, 133
Valley of Va., 24
Vineyards, 76
Virginia Gazette, 225
Virginia ships, 28
Vobe, Jane, 145, 197

Wager, Anne, Mrs., 139-148
Wallace, Betty, 49
Waller, Benjamin, 53, 62, 132
Waring, James, Rev., 138
Washington, George, 99, 219, 231
Watch, Night, 208
Waters, William, 54
Weatherburn, Henry, 54, 63